DATE DUE

FEB 1 7 2014	
	N

GAYLORD	PRINTED IN U.S.A.

Osama Bin Laden:

The last days

BRANDON FRANKLIN HURST

ISBN: 978-1-926893-77-8

Cover design: François Turgeon
Text design and composition: Benjamin Roland

Cover photo:
© Rex Features

Published in collaboration with Cogito America Inc
and Creative Media Funds LLC.

www.cogitomedias.com

Printed and Bound in the United States of America

TABLE OF CONTENTS

PART ONE: TEN YEARS ON   **11**

KILL OR CAPTURE   13

CHASING THE GHOST   21

BLACK HAWK DOWN   33

ESCAPE FROM ABBOTTABAD   41

THE WAR OF WORDS   49

PART TWO: BIRTH OF A TERRORIST   **61**

THE METEORIC RISE OF SHEIKH BIN LADEN   63

THE GAP OPENS   71

PART THREE: JIHADI   **83**

THE ALLY OF THE CIA   85

BUSINESS AND PLEASURE   91

THE WORLD TURNS   95

AT HOME AND ABROAD   101

PART FOUR: THE TWIN TOWERS   **115**

AL QAEDA'S MASTER PLAN   117

THE DAY THE WORLD CHANGED   125

FIGHTING BACK   137

CONCLUSION: AFTERMATH   **145**

"THE PEARL HARBOR OF THE 21ST CENTURY"   147

THE WAR ON TERROR   151

NO GOING BACK   161

POSTSCRIPT :   **167**
THE ARAB SPRING AND THE FUTURE OF AL QAEDA

BIBLIOGRAPHY   **173**

Brandon Franklin Hurst

Perhaps he really is enjoying Paradise and the rewards that martyrs are traditionally believed to receive in the afterlife. But the truth is likely more prosaic: an anonymous grave at the bottom of the North Arabian Sea and a fast-closing chapter in the history books of the late 20th and early 21st centuries. Whether justice comes in merely earthly terms or has eternal implications, it was served for Osama bin Laden on May 1, 2011.

TEN YEARS ON

KILL OR CAPTURE

THE TWO MODIFIED Black Hawk helicopters thudded softly through the night sky over the tense and lawless Taliban territory that lies between Afghanistan and Pakistan. Like most helicopters, a Black Hawk will usually make a thundering racket as its rotors whip through the air, but these were something new – something so secret they had never been seen before. If it hadn't been of utmost importance for the mission, public knowledge of their existence would not have been risked.

Like the top-secret craft in which they flew, it is likely that little will be widely revealed about the twenty-five elite U.S. Navy SEALs who were deployed early that morning from the helicopters to their target destination, a compound in the town of Abbottabad a few miles from the capital of Pakistan. At some point during the mission, probably all of them recalled the time almost ten years earlier when two other aircraft had made iconic and terrible history, that time in broad daylight over the Manhattan skyline. It is inconceivable that between them they did not have friends and family who died in the terrorist attacks on the Twin Towers on September 11, 2001.

Their mission had been announced to them several weeks earlier, after which they had undergone a period of intense training in preparation. It was code-named Operation Neptune Spear. Navy SEALs are tasked with some of the toughest and most important work on the planet, but they recognized the special significance of this occasion. "They were told, 'We think we found Osama bin Laden,' one official recalled, 'and your job is to kill him.'" Their reaction had been to break into cheers and applause.

The *Associated Press* has cited other U.S. officials who have stated that the operation was "a kill-or-capture mission, since the U.S. doesn't kill unarmed people trying to surrender." After the raid had successfully been completed, John O. Brennan, the White House's counterterrorism advisor, told the press, "If we had the opportunity to take bin Laden alive, if he didn't present any threat, the individuals involved were able and prepared to do that." Nevertheless, they conceded that "it was clear from the beginning that whoever was behind those walls had no intention of surrendering." In other words, giving him the benefit of the doubt wasn't an option.

Altogether, a team of seventy-nine commandos were involved, including those twenty-five SEALs who went in on the ground and engaged the enemy. However, the circle had been kept deliberately small to avoid any unnecessary chance of compromise. Even high-level White House officials didn't know what was going on in the minutes after midnight on that day: President Obama had been fanatically careful not to endanger the men who flew into Pakistan under cover of night or to jeopardize the success of their crucial mission.

The SEALs flew from Bagram Air Base in Afghanistan to Jalalabad before making the crossing into Pakistan. They were equipped with versatile M4 carbines, as well as handguns and night-vision goggles. The state-of-the-art equipment was standard issue, but the aircraft in which they flew was something so cutting-edge that it had never been heard of before outside of elite military circles. The craft had been supplied by the so-called Night Stalkers, the 160th Special Operations Aviation

Regiment. The Black Hawk helicopter was first acquired by the U.S. Army in 1978. The standard model has a crew of four – two pilots, a flight engineer and a gunner – and can hold up to 11 fully equipped soldiers. Its maximum takeoff weight is 22,000 pounds, and it is capable of carrying an additional 9,000 pounds of external load by sling. Its top speed is 184 mph. This already formidable craft, the workhorse of the Afghan and Iraq conflicts, had been upgraded with stealth capabilities – probably the reason the mission got so far without Pakistani officials even realizing it. The alterations included a modified tail boom, plus a change in design and a covering on the rear rotors that would vastly reduce external noise. "Helicopters make a very distinctive percussive rotor sound, which is caused by their rotor blades and if you can blend that down, of course that makes a noise that is much less likely to be heard and much more likely to blend into any background noise that there is," said Bill Sweetman, editor-In-Chief of *Defense Technology International*. They were also covered in a special radar-absorbent material, similar to the type used in stealth fighter planes. Dan Gouré, a former Department of Defense official and vice president of the Lexington Institute, concluded that the result was something never seen before. "This is a first," he commented. "You wouldn't know that it was coming right at you. And that's what's important, because these are coming in fast and low, and if they aren't sounding like they're coming right at you, you might not even react until it's too late... That was clearly part of the success."

The Night Stalkers also provided three Chinook helicopters as backup – which would be required after one of the Black Hawks went down in action and had to be destroyed. In addition, the Air Force had a full complement of search-and-rescue aircraft at the ready, and the SEALs would have the support of both drones and manned fighter jets.

The two helicopters flew in low over the mountains and in little moonlight to avoid detection before they reached their target. Their stealth modifications meant that they were almost silent until directly overhead, and harder to detect by radar than earlier models. Due to the extra weight of the stealth equipment, the SEALs' own gear had been finely calculated to ensure the aircraft were not overloaded.

They arrived thirty minutes after midnight, local time – as the Western world was going about its Sunday business with no knowledge of what was unfolding several thousand miles away. But then, even bin Laden and his closest neighbors had little warning until the Black Hawks were overhead. Nearby residents reported hearing a series of loud explosions a few minutes apart, and then one enormous explosion that rocked their houses. The lights went on and off and there was the sound of gunshots, but that didn't last long. Within a couple of minutes it had stopped. Some of the residents in the area had apparently been instructed to turn off their lights, raising the question of who had told them. The Pakistani security forces were the most obvious candidate, but the language used had been simple Pashto – not the chief language of the area. It is possible that covert U.S. personnel were paving the way for their colleagues' work.

President Obama and his security team were following the progress of Operation Neptune Spear in real time from the White House, though it is unclear in what form they were receiving updates – at key points, they were completely in the dark, with no operational live feed coming from the SEALs. The importance of this mission was abundantly clear to the president, who had been closely involved in its planning for the past eight months, since the main intelligence-gathering report on the compound. He had met with national security advisors several times over the weeks preceding the raid, honing the plan from the many different options that were presented to him. In those weeks, he had considered and rejected numerous easier options. One of the first was simply to bomb the compound, using a B-2 stealth bomber to drop a 2,000-pound device to wipe it from the face of the earth. However effective such a strategy might be, it would almost inevitably result in civilian casualties, and would in any case give no proof that bin Laden had been inside. After almost ten years of uncertainty as to his location, it would be unbearable not to know whether he was still at large or whether the raid had been successful.

Another option was a joint raid, using American SEALs, but informing Pakistani operatives only hours beforehand to avoid leaking information. This, too, was held to constitute unacceptable risk. In the event, the best way to go about the operation would be to carry it out entirely under the radar, without the knowledge of the Pakistani intelligence agencies – until it became unavoidable. The alternative would be to allow the real possibility of information reaching bin Laden himself, at which point he would disappear and the U.S. would maybe lose its last chance to bring him to justice. So President Obama came to the decision that sending in a team of U.S. SEALs was the best way to ensure success, whatever the increased risks. The men in the two helicopters had been instructed to avoid engagement with any Pakistani police or military personnel if possible, although as a last resort they had authorization to open fire on them. To allow for this unfortunate eventuality, he had increased the size of the team to improve their chances of escaping alive.

President Obama gave final authorization to the CIA at 8:20 a.m. on April 29. Operation Neptune Spear was due to take place that day, but was postponed a day due to adverse weather – 24 tense, but calculated hours during which forces outside of human control could make all the difference to the mission, but also during which human error or malicious intent could have irrevocably compromised the operation.

Obama witnessed the proceedings in the Pakistani compound in real time from the Situation Room of the White House. A seventh-floor conference room at the CIA headquarters at Langley, Virginia had been turned into a command center; from there, CIA director Leon Panetta ensured that the president and his advisors were kept up to date with every possible detail – although, he later said, there were around twenty minutes after the SEALs entered the compound that they "really didn't know just exactly what was going on." That comment suggests that any live feed they may have been using was either switched off or failed at the crucial moment.

Obama would later say that the forty minutes of the raid itself were among the longest of his life. For minutes, for those men and women at Langley and for the SEALs on the ground in Pakistan, the situation lay on a knife-edge. Obama refrained from telling his family and some of his closest aides about what he had ordered. Indeed, he was not certain – even at this point – that bin Laden was even at the Abbottabad compound when the helicopters landed. The evidence was circumstantial and he considered the odds to be only just in favor of bin Laden's presence. Either way, it must have occurred to him that this could be the defining moment of his presidency, and a crucial watershed: up until that point he had been viewed as weak on international relations after eight jingoistic Bush years and two wars in the Middle East. Some critics had questioned his nerve, suggesting he was soft on foreign policy and had no stomach for the kind of decisions that were required of the president of the most powerful country in the world. But if it went wrong, if SEALs died, then he had made the wrong choice: why did he not call in the much safer air strike?

Embarrassment was another potential risk: what if the compound hadn't housed bin Laden after all, but belonged to another wealthy man? In an interview the following week, he credited the Special Forces responsible for the operation with doing "an extraordinary job, with just the slenderest of bits of information."

"At the end of the day, this was still a 55/45 situation. I mean, we could not say definitively that bin Laden was there," he said. "If it turns out that it's a wealthy prince from Dubai who's in this compound and we've sent Special Forces in, we've got problems." Those doubts were expanded and multiplied by the few officials who did know about Neptune Spear, but he says he welcomed their input as he considered the merits of 'safer' options, like an air strike. "The fact that there were some who voiced doubts about this approach was invaluable, because it meant the plan was sharper, it meant that we had thought through all of our options, it meant that when I finally did make the decision I was making it based on the very best information," he concluded. "It wasn't as if any of the folks who were voicing doubts were voicing something that I wasn't already running through in my own head."

Nevertheless, Obama regretted that he could not cast the net wider, asking some top aides for their opinions. And the Pakistani authorities – who might rightly be horrified about an unauthorized and deadly operation on their soil – were completely off the table. "I didn't tell most people here in the White House. I didn't tell my own family. It was that important for us to maintain operational security. If I'm not revealing to some of my closest aides what we're doing, then I sure as heck am not going to be revealing it to folks who I don't know.'

The knowledge of the impending operation had eaten away at him as he went about the task of filling in the extra hours before the weather cleared, making the mission possible. He admitted his difficulty in keeping his mind on those important but seemingly trivial tasks – seeing the damage from the recent tornados, speaking at the launch of the space shuttle and giving an address at the White House Correspondents' Dinner – an occasion where he managed to inject some levity into the proceedings, despite the weight on his mind.

And then, nearly ten years after the attacks on the Twin Towers and eight months after the intelligence of bin Laden's location had been obtained, the moment came. Images of the president in the control center at Langley show a tense, anxious face focusing entirely on the feed of information. And yet, he said, information was limited; there were "large chunks of time in which all we were doin' was just waiting."

"It was the longest forty minutes of my life," he added, "with the possible exception of when Sasha got meningitis when she was three months old and I was waiting for the doctor to tell me that she was all right."

The mission was supposed to take just thirty minutes once the SEALs reached their destination. In the event, in the face of unforeseen circumstances, including the crash of one of the stealth-modified Black Hawks, it took thirty-eight minutes. But those interminable minutes – even for the president and his advisors in the information-starved Situation Room – were nothing compared to the ten years of near-silence from bin Laden himself. He had remained hidden for almost a decade, evident only in a series of taunting broadcasts in which his location was never clear. Only once in the time since 9/11 had U.S. forces even come close to finding him: only once, three months after the atrocities in Manhattan, had friends and relatives of those who died had a chance of closure.

CHASING THE GHOST

OSAMA BIN LADEN might have finally been located in an expensive residential compound, but he was no stranger to hardship. In the years before 9/11, with the help of his significant wealth and equipment from his family's construction business, he had developed a large network of caves and tunnels high in the mountains of Tora Bora in eastern Afghanistan, 14,000 feet above sea-level. The mountains are hazardous and obscure, offering the perfect hiding place for anyone who knew them well enough. Just miles from Pakistan, the complex of passages and dwellings also offered the ideal way to melt away as troops moved into the area to threaten his safety.

'Dalton Fury' – the pen name of the Delta Force commander who later wrote a book, *Kill bin Laden*, about his experiences – recounted how his soldiers located bin Laden in the mountains, but could not prevent him from disappearing into the secret trails and pathways among the peaks, vanishing from public sight for years longer. Fury confessed his anguish to *60 Minutes* at allowing the Al Qaeda chief to slip between his fingers. Worst, he said, was knowing where the terrorist was, but being impotent to apprehend him. "Our job was to go find him, capture or kill him, and we knew the writing on the wall was to kill him because nobody wanted to bring Osama bin Laden back to stand trial in the United States somewhere," he told the interviewer.

On one occasion, Fury's forces were closing around bin Laden's band of fighters, but had to stop the offensive because they did not have the support of Afghan troops. His team of fifty Delta Force men was pitted against 1,000 of bin Laden's soldiers. They had no chance without the Afghan fighters that the U.S. relied on at the time. However, many Afghan soldiers saw the terrorist chief as a hero, and refused to co-operate.

Not long afterward, Delta soldiers literally saw bin Laden with their own eyes, only to have him somehow escape the bombardment to come. "The operation Jackal team observed 50 men moving into a cave that they hadn't seen before. The Mujahideen said they saw an individual, a taller fellow, wearing a camouflage jacket. Everybody put two and two together, 'okay, that's got to be Osama bin Laden egressing from the battlefield.' They called up every available bomb in the air, took control of the airspace. And they dropped several hours of bombs on the cave he went into. We believe, it was our opinion at the time, that he died inside that cave."

It was not to be the case. Somehow, he had escaped the firestorm – although, according to Fury, he was not unscathed by the attack. American searches scoured the area, but could find no sign of the body. Confirmation of his survival came some time later, when the intermittent trickle of video and audio messages to the outside world began again. Fury believes that he was wounded by shrapnel from one of the bombs, but was hidden by Al Qaeda sympathizers until he was well enough to be carried off into Pakistan. "We believe a gentleman brought him in – a gentleman, him and his family were supporting Al Qaeda during the battle. They were providing food, ammo, water. We think he went to that house, received medical attention for a few days then, and then we believe they put him in a vehicle and moved him back across the pass," he was quoted.

It was the closest anyone would get for another nine years, when the CIA finally pinpointed his whereabouts and Obama authorized the kill-or-capture mission to Abbottabad. During that time, bin Laden earned and re-earned the nickname 'Elvis' given to him by American intelligence services, due to the frequent and unlikely sightings reported all over the world. Until, that is, the fall of 2010, when the possibility was raised in an intelligence briefing with the president that the FBI's Most Wanted man was alive and well and hiding with no great degree of effort in a large and comfortable compound some distance from the Pakistani capital. It took eight months to confirm it, and another one to prepare the mission.

U.S. intelligence services had left no stone unturned in their hunt for the terrorist. The details of their efforts read like an elaborate puzzle, or a complicated computer game where steps forward are painstakingly made by piecing together existing information obtained by every means necessary. The vital piece of the puzzle was provided by the couriers who had been Osama bin Laden's only real link to the outside world for so long.

Back in 1998, Operation Infinite Reach had resulted in U.S. missile strikes being launched against bin Laden's bases in Afghanistan and Sudan. The authorities had gained the information of his whereabouts by tracking one of his associates' satellite phones. Having learned the hard way, bin Laden no longer used phones. Unlike the majority of the world today, for bin Laden technology was not a link to the outside world: it was a potential death sentence. Instead, he used couriers, a handful of trusted and strategic men who would carry information to and from the Al Qaeda leader. This way, even some of the highest-ranking officials in Al Qaeda did not know his identity.

His favorite courier was a man known to most of the world only by the *nom de guerre* Abu Ahmed al-Kuwaiti. (His real name has not been released by the CIA, who tracked him diligently for years.) In al-Kuwaiti, bin Laden placed his entire trust. Although he never willingly or intentionally betrayed that trust, it is fitting that it was through his movements that the Most Wanted man in the world was tracked and ultimately brought to justice.

Al-Kuwaiti was a Pakistani-born Pashtun who had grown up in Kuwait and consequently spoke both Arabic and Pashto (in, it is said, a cultivated urban accent). Moreover, he had been mentored by none other than Khalid Sheikh Mohammed – the Al Qaeda kingpin and lead planner on the September 11 attacks. Al-Kuwaiti had supposedly assisted the hijackers by giving them IT training.

It is easy to see why al-Kuwaiti was useful to bin Laden. Bilingual in Arabic and Pashto, he could bridge the gap between the Arab-speaking members of Al Qaeda and the local people in the stronghold of the Pashtun region between Afghanistan and Pakistan.

A leaked WikiLeaks document reported that a Guantanamo detainee by the name of Mohamedou Ould Salahi had claimed that – like bin Laden himself – al-Kuwaiti had been injured during the Battle of Tora Bora in December 2001, but unlike his commander, who had died of his wounds. According to this document, Abu Ahmed al-Kuwaiti was "a mid-level Al Qaeda operative who facilitated the movement and safe haven of senior Al Qaeda members and families." When the CIA learned that al-Kuwaiti was alive after all, they pulled apart every strand they could find, knowing that he could be a vital lead back to the very top of Al Qaeda.

It took years to put the pieces together. The work started with what have been called 'aggressive interrogations' or 'enhanced interrogations' in black sites outside of the U.S., as well as at the notorious Guantanamo Bay. These black sites were overseas prisons, off the radar to the public and known only to a handful of officials who oversaw them and squeezed their inmates for information over a period of months and years.

As with so many other aspects of the bin Laden story, there are details which have not yet been made public, and may never be. But some things are known. We know the identities of some of the detainees who were interrogated, and we know a bit about how they were coerced into giving up the information they did – including the identity of the courier who would finally led the U.S. forces to the compound in Abbottabad in the early hours of the first of May.

"Multiple sources of intelligence led us to where we are," MSNBC quoted a senior U.S. intelligence official – who, like many others in his position, only gave a statement on the strict condition of anonymity. "Key information was gleaned from detainees and that detainee reporting provided insight into the courier network." Human rights groups have criticized the methods used, and questioned whether they provide reliable, usable evidence. The conclusion to be drawn from this episode appears to be – sometimes. There is a limit to what any human can withstand, but many of these sources were martyrs willing to die for their cause. The only question was whether there was something worse than death that the authorities could use to extract information from them. In some cases, the answer appears to have been no – or, at least, the process took far longer than seems possible and involved too much false information along the way. In other cases, it was faster and more reliable.

One way or another, it was through these "enhanced interrogations," carried out far from public scrutiny and U.S. law, that the authorities gained a foothold into that most important member of bin Laden's network, the courier al-Kuwaiti. One of the crucial sources of that information was a detainee by the name of Mohammed al-Qahtani, a candidate for the identity of the notorious "20th hijacker" of 9/11.

Of the four planes that were captured and turned against the U.S. on September 11, 2001, three were taken by bands of five hijackers. The fourth plane, United Airlines Flight 93, contained only four hijackers. In the days that followed the atrocities, speculation was rife that there had not been nineteen men directly involved in the plot that day, but twenty – one of whom had been unable to join the other members of his crew.

The Saudi-born al-Qahtani had tried to enter the U.S. on August 3, 2001 – just five weeks before 9/11. It later transpired that the lead hijacker, Mohamed Atta, went to meet him at Orlando Airport in Florida off his flight from Dubai. But al-Qahtani was not allowed into the country. His one-way ticket and the fact that he carried only $2,800 in cash raised suspicions. Airport officials deported him back to Dubai, believing that he intended to stay on as an illegal immigrant. He later returned to Pakistan. The mistake bought al-Qahtani four more months of freedom, and – to date – ten years of incarceration and torture. He was picked up again at Tora Bora in December 2001 and sent to Guantanamo Bay. For ten months he protested his innocence, giving a false name – he was, he claimed, only coincidentally in the same areas as the Al Qaeda chief when the battle raged. He was pursuing an interest in falconry. It was all a mistake.

It was ten months before his fingerprints linked him to the airport in the U.S., and his visit was linked to surveillance tapes in which co-conspirator Mohammed Atta's car was apparently visible. And so, having been identified as a plausible candidate for the 20th hijacker, the torture began.

The process took place over a period of seven weeks between November 2002 and January 2003, though he was kept in isolation until that April. Some of the "enhanced interrogation" techniques involved included forcing al-Qahtani to wear a bra and leading him around on a dog's leash. Dogs are considered unclean in Islam, and keeping a dog as a pet is forbidden. He was also forced to perform dog tricks. This humiliation was used in conjunction with less sophisticated techniques: he was exposed to temperatures so low and for so long that he twice ended up in hospital with bradycardia. This condition – literally the slowness of heart – is typically defined as the heart rate falling below sixty beats per minute, although it is rarely dangerous unless it drops below fifty beats. At lower rates, the heart cannot pump enough oxygen around the body, which can lead to faintness, loss of consciousness, heart attack and death. Al-Qahtani's heart rate dropped to thirty-five beats per minute at one point.

On at least one occasion, he was threatened with a real dog, a military animal named Zeus. Prolonged isolation, nudity, physical threats, exposure to the cold and sleep deprivation achieved what more conventional questioning could not. Nevertheless, there would be fallout for the administration at the time. During the closing months of President Bush's presidency, Susan Crawford – chief of the U.S. military commissions at the time, tasked with deciding whether to bring detainees to trial – rejected the prosecution of Qahtani because of what had taken place at Guantanamo. "We tortured Qahtani," she told the *Washington Post*. "His treatment met the legal definition of torture. And that's why I did not refer the case."

"For one hundred sixty days his only contact was with the interrogators," she said. "Forty-eight of fifty-four consecutive days of eighteen-to-twenty-hour interrogations. Standing naked in front of a female agent. Subject to strip searches. And insults to his mother and sister." Crawford was the first official in the Bush administration to state in public that a Guantanamo detainee had been subject to torture. Incredibly, it was not the individual techniques themselves that were the problem, but their prolonged use and combination. "The techniques they used were all authorized, but the manner in which they applied them was overly aggressive and too persistent... You think of torture, you think of some horrendous physical act done to an individual. This was not any one particular act; this was just a combination of things that had a medical impact on him, that hurt his health. It was abusive and uncalled for. And coercive. Clearly coercive. It was that medical impact that pushed me over the edge," she said.

President Bush denied that torture had occurred. "The United States does not torture. It's against our laws, and it's against our values," he claimed in September 2006, after a number of significant detainees had been moved to Guantanamo Bay CIA black sites. Vice President Cheney added, "I think on the left wing of the Democratic Party, there are some people who believe that we really tortured." Crawford was under few illusions. "I sympathize with the intelligence gatherers in those days after 9/11, not knowing what was coming next and trying to gain information to keep us safe," *MSNBC* quoted her. "But there still has to be a line that we should not cross. And unfortunately, what this has done, I think, has tainted everything going forward... I was upset by it. I was embarrassed by it. If we tolerate this and allow it, then how can we object when our servicemen and women, or others in foreign service, are captured and subjected to the same techniques? How can we complain? Where is our moral authority to complain? Well, we may have lost it." Crawford dismissed the charges against him of war crimes in May 2008. Six months later, military prosecutors stated that they intended to file charges again, this time based on later interrogations that did not involved such harsh methods.

In the weeks following his detention in Guantanamo Bay, al-Qahtani had admitted to a number of crimes, to meeting Osama bin Laden on several occasions, and to having been sent to the U.S. by Khalid Sheikh Mohammed, the master planner of the 9/11 attacks. Crawford's decision not to prosecute left her in a quandary. What should they do with him? "There's no doubt in my mind he would've been on one of those planes had he gained access to the country in August 2001," she said. "He's a muscle hijacker... He's a very dangerous man. What do you do with him now if you don't charge him and try him? I would be hesitant to say, 'Let him go.'" To date, al-Qahtani remains in Guantanamo Bay, his legal status unclear.

Those interrogations turned up the name of the courier, Abu Ahmed al-Kuwaiti – information that matched the statements given by another notorious Al Qaeda operative, Khalid Sheikh

Mohammed. According to the findings of the 9/11 Commission, 'KSM,' as he is widely known, was "the principal architect of the 9/11 attacks." He was captured in a joint mission between Pakistani intelligence officers and the CIA in Rawalpindi, Pakistan, in March 2003.

If al-Qahtani's treatment could be described as torture, there was no doubt about Khalid Sheikh Mohammed's. He was subjected to the notorious and controversial technique of waterboarding multiple times and for prolonged periods in the same month that he was captured.

Waterboarding is a simple, but brutally effective technique. There are variations, but generally speaking the suspect is restrained and held down on their backs. The face is typically covered with a cloth, blindfolding them and wrapping around the mouth and nose. Water is then poured over the face, flooding into the mouth and nose and immediately creating a gag reflex and the sensation of drowning. Physical and psychological implications are extensive, and range from immediate to delayed onset, months or even years after the event. Lung and brain damage from oxygen deprivation are possible, as is death if the process is not halted. Suspects have been known to suffer broken bones – not from their captors, but from the violence of their struggling as they try to escape the sensation. Trained interrogators know all the ways that their subjects try to avoid or delay the agony, and have developed effective ways of circumventing them. Few people last more than a few seconds without begging for mercy.

A CIA memo on guidelines for waterboarding reads as follows: "…where authorized, it may be used for two 'sessions' per day of up to two hours. During a session, water may be applied up to six times for ten seconds or longer (but never more than forty seconds). In a twenty-four-hour period, a detainee may be subjected to up to twelve minutes of water application. Additionally, the waterboard may be used on as many as five days during a thirty-day approval period."

The *New York Times* quoted a former C.I.A. officer, John Kiriakou, who told a number of news organizations in 2007 that another detainee considered to be of high value, Abu Zubaydah, had "undergone waterboarding for only hirty-five seconds before agreeing to tell everything he knew." Nevertheless, he was waterboarded 83 times within the space of a month.

When it came to Khalid Sheikh Mohammed, the CIA apparently threw away the rulebook. One hundred and eighty-three times in March 2003 he was waterboarded. One hundred and eighty-three times he struggled, choking violently and thrashing for his life against his restraints. One hundred and eighty-three times he gasped air into his lungs at the end of the process and told his interrogators whatever they wanted to know, and more. Indeed, some CIA agents expressed concern that much of what he said was simply "white noise," either intended to mislead his captors or simply to buy him time before the next occasion he was strapped down and subjected to simulated drowning.

Nevertheless, for all the "white noise" the list of plots with which KSM has reliably been linked is impressive. 9/11 ("I was responsible for the 9/11 operation, from A to Z," he confessed at one hearing), the 1993 bombing of the World Trade Center, the Bali nightclub bombings, Richard Reid's "shoe bomb" attempt to destroy a plane, beheading *Wall Street Reporter* journalist Daniel Pearl, plots to kill Bill Clinton, the Pope, and many other high-profile figures and destroy many other high-value targets – these were just a few of his involvements.

And it was also from KSM that the U.S. gained the *nom de guerre* of one of Osama bin Laden's most trusted couriers, the man known as Abu Ahmed al-Kuwaiti. Still, he refused to give the man's true name. Perhaps Mohammed didn't know his real name at all, or perhaps he held out on his captors after all, through all the interrogation. "They waterboarded KSM one hundred and eighty-three times and he still didn't give the guy up," one former counterterrorism official stated. "Come on. And you want to tell me that enhanced interrogation techniques worked?"

It took years to figure out who al-Kuwaiti really was, including information collected from numerous other detainees in Guantanamo and black sites around the world. "Four years ago, we uncovered his identity," one senior U.S. official admitted after Operation Neptune Spear concluded. Two years after that, they managed to trace him and his brother to Pakistan. The final, crucial break came in August 2010, when the location of the courier was finally pinpointed accurately. He had been found in a large compound in Abbottabad, some thirty-five miles north of the Pakistani capital Islamabad, and went locally by the name of Arshad Khan. That was when the mission could finally begin in earnest.

BLACK HAWK DOWN

THE TWO HELICOPTERS emerged from the darkness over Abbottabad – a place known as the "City of Pines." In reality, it is a small agricultural town in the fertile hill-country of northwest Pakistan. Its population is only 120,000, but it forms a hub for many of its neighboring villages. However, it is not only farmers who live in Abbottabad. The town is home to a military garrison, and one of Pakistan's most celebrated training academies. Osama bin Laden had been found living half a mile away from the Pakistani equivalent of America's West Point or Britain's Sandhurst – a uniquely bold move, and one that could have proven disastrous for any foreign forces that could have per chance been in the area. Pakistan's army chief regularly visits the academy for graduation parades and other events. Bilal Town, the district in which the compound is located, is home to numerous retired high-level military personnel, and it is probable that the area would have been protected by heightened security, checkpoints and constant military presence.

The compound the SEALs arrived at after thirty minutes in the air was roughly triangular, and was valued by U.S. agents at roughly $1 million. It was far larger and worth significantly more than any of the houses surrounding it. The wide area in which the SEALs planned to hit the ground had walls over sixteen feet high, topped with barbed wire and CCTV cameras.

For all its grandeur, it wasn't clear how many people would be found at the compound, and therefore the level of resistance was an unknown. Electricity bills showed that the inhabitants used almost no power – enough to run the lights, and the small TV set that bin Laden used to keep track of the news. But that wasn't a good indication of how many of his family members or fighters would be there. Even before he was forced to go on the run, the wealthy Saudi-born businessman was known for living a surprisingly austere life, and could happily get by without the creature comforts afforded by electricity.

The original plan was supposed to take exactly thirty minutes. In the event, it took thirty-eight, the SEALs requiring a lean eight minutes extra to improvise after the harsh conditions forced a helicopter down. The intention was that one team of SEALs would fast rope down from the chopper – a technique where the troops slide down the rope with gloved hands, like descending a fireman's pole. It is faster, but more dangerous than rappelling, since there is no figure-of-eight or descender mechanism to attach the person to the rope. Whilst that team approached from the air, the second helicopter would land in the compound and the second team would penetrate the building from the ground.

Up until that point, everything had gone according to plan. The pilot had negotiated the mountains without detection, and found the compound without incident. But as he hovered over the compound to drop the SEALs onto the roof, he lost control. In the hot and high-altitude conditions of Pakistan, the air is thinner than at lower and colder altitudes, and the helicopter's rotors provide lower levels of lift. The high compound walls added to the problem, preventing the rotors' downward wash from dispersing. The result was a phenomenon known as a vortex ring state, whereby the rotors recycle the air they have just propelled downward – moving downward through downward-moving air, destroying their lift capacity. It is a hazard well-known to helicopter pilots in Iraq and Afghanistan, where high temperatures, high altitudes and sandstorms can wreck the otherwise reliable lifting power of a large helicopter. Over the past ten years, dozens of such craft have either been shot down or crashed when they encountered adverse flying conditions.

The effect was almost catastrophic, with the downward force requiring the pilot to make a hard landing in the compound rather than hovering above it. As he did so, the tail of the stealth helicopter smashed into one of the compound's walls, snapping one of the rotors. The helicopter immediately rolled onto its side. That could have been the end of the mission, and the death of everyone on board, but the pilot's lightning-fast reactions quickly brought the craft back into a controlled crash, with the nose burying into the floor of the compound. Seconds later the team was outside of the now-useless craft, its unharmed crew running to join the SEALs from the second helicopter that had safely landed nearby.

The twenty-five SEALs set their minds on their target – a large, concrete building in the center of the compound, three storys high and set in a courtyard protected from sight and intrusion by further walls. Although this was the first time they had been there in person, they had trained extensively on replicas of the compound in the U.S. When the stakes were so high, there was no room for error and they would have memorized the layout until they knew it like their own homes. They knew the locations of the security gates and any guards who would man them; they knew they would have to scale or otherwise breach a number of walls to reach their target; they knew that the owner was so fanatical about his privacy that he had no phone or Internet connection, and that he insisted that his rubbish was burned within its perimeter rather than left out for collection.

What happened next happened fast and accounts are confused. Again, it is likely that full details will never properly be released, and the official version has already been revised at least once.

But from the accounts available, the best reconstruction goes as follows:

Using explosives to blast through the walls of the courtyard – probably the noise that residents later reported hearing in the night – the SEALs left the two helicopters behind them and gained access to the large house in the center. As they emerged into the open, the first and only armed resistance occurred. Abu Ahmed al-Kuwaiti was hiding behind the door of a guesthouse next to the main building. Perhaps he realized that he, bin Laden's most trusted courier, had been the means by which the CIA had tracked the terrorist chief. But in the dark and the early hours of the morning, he would have had few cues to alert him to the fact that it was an American mission. He probably acted in desperation, knowing that he had no chance of survival under such superior and organized fire power, and that his only option was to buy time and honor in some small way by killing the aggressors before they killed him and his mentor – or else, worse, captured them alive. He aimed his AK-47 and fired, sparking a brief gunfight during which his own wife was killed in the cross-fire. Seconds later, he too, was shot dead.

The way was now clear for them to move into the building, the second team of SEALs climbed the stairs, knowing that they could encounter further armed resistance at every step. Almost immediately, on the first floor, they met another man, shooting him before he could reach the weapon that lay nearby. It would later turn out to be al-Kuwaiti's brother. Ensuring that the floor was clear they swiftly progressed to the staircase up to the second and third floors, where they knew that bin Laden – if he lived here – must surely be. A second man rushed toward them on the staircase, but was shot as quickly as the first. This one would turn out to be Khalid bin Laden, their ultimate target's twenty-two-year-old son.

The climax of the mission occurred twenty minutes after the SEALs had landed in the compound. Climbing the stairs, they saw a face looking down at them from the third floor – a face that was instantly recognizable from news broadcasts the world over from the last ten years. It was final confirmation that the man known as "the pacer" – so-called because in secret CIA footage of the compound, the tall figure could be seen steadily pacing around – was the man they hunted. One of the SEALs fired a shot, but bin Laden ducked out of sight.

Now that their quarry was fully aware of his situation, there was little time left. The SEALs knew that within seconds bin Laden would procure a weapon and possibly hostages, vastly complicating the operation and significantly reducing the odds of escaping with minimal bloodshed – to themselves or anyone else in the building. They stormed the final flight of stairs, not knowing when they reached the top whether they would meet an unarmed man or a deadly hail of bullets. Worse, they knew it was quite possible that he would be prepared in the most terrifying way he knew, one which he and other extremists had masterminded and practiced across the world in many terrorist attacks. What if he were wearing a suicide vest, detonating it and killing himself and everyone in the room with the press of a button?

Following the retreating figure into his bedroom, the SEALs tasked with his death-or-capture finally gained the first proper look at bin Laden by western forces for nearly a decade. The tall, thin, heavily-bearded man was wearing *kurta paijama* – the long, loose fitting shirt and pants traditional in Afghanistan and Pakistan. He was unarmed, but there were two guns nearby: the AK-47 assault rifle favored by desert fighters for its power and simplicity, and a 9-millimeter Makarov semi-automatic pistol – another simple, cheap and powerful weapon used in the past by Soviet police and still popular in the U.S. today.

The immediate distraction came not from bin Laden himself but from two young children. This was the nightmare scenario: that innocent members of his family, too young to understand anything of his history or the reasons their father was being hunted, would be caught in the crossfire, possibly buying bin Laden enough time to escape or kill the intruders. The first SEAL into the room snatched the two children up and bundled them out of the way. As the second member of the team entered the room, a young woman rushed toward him. He fired a shot, hitting her in the leg and effectively immobilizing her. A third member of the team, his path now finally clear, took aim with his M4 and fired a fast and effective double-tap: a primary shot to the torso followed by an immediate second shot to the face – on this occasion, one bullet in the chest and a second just above the left eye.

They were the final shots to be fired in the compound that night. Altogether, four men and one woman had died: the courier al-Kuwaiti, his wife and brother, bin Laden's son Khalid and the Al Qaeda chief himself. Two women had been injured. They turned out to be his fifth wife, the twenty-year-old Amal Ahmed Abdul Fatah, and his twelve year-old daughter by another wife, who was struck by a ricochet or by debris in the foot. She also witnessed her father being killed at close range.

And finally, from his vantage point thousands of miles away in the Situation Room of the White House, President Obama heard the words he had been waiting for during that period of information blackout that had lasted for most of the time the SEALs were in the compound: "Geronimo EKIA," short for 'Enemy Killed In Action'.

Bin Laden had not fired a shot, nor held a weapon, and he had not attempted to communicate with the forces that stormed the building. It is likely that there was no opportunity for him to do any of those – and the SEALs were not about to give him the chance. CIA director Leon Panetta later told *PBS Newshour*, "Obviously, under the rules of engagement, if he had in fact thrown up his hands, surrendered and didn't appear to be representing any kind of threat, then they were to capture him. But they had full authority to kill him." John Brennan, Obama's Chief Counterterrorism Advisor, explained, "The concern was that bin

Laden would oppose any type of capture operation. Indeed, he did. It was a firefight. He, therefore, was killed in that firefight."

So who was the man who finally pulled the trigger on the world's most wanted man, killing the terrorist responsible for thousands of deaths in the U.S. and across the world? It is highly improbable that his identity will be revealed any time soon. In fact, releasing to the public any of the identities of the SEALs who entered the compound in Abbottabad that night – or any of the other men who formed the backup teams – would constitute an unacceptable risk, since it would immediately make them a prime target for an Al Qaeda backlash. It would also mean they were effectively barred from taking part in any future covert missions, removing their considerable experience and expertise from the fight against terrorism. For this reason, no one outside of tight military and high-level political circles knows who arrested Saddam or brought down some of the other top figures in the Taliban or Al Qaeda. Nevertheless, speculates the *Washington Post*, there are clues as to his identity and the kind of person he is likely to be. The *Post* interviewed three former Navy SEALs with the aim of filling in some of the blanks of the unnamed and faceless hero.

"He's likely between the ages of twenty-six and thirty-three," it explained. "He'll be old enough to have had time to hurdle the extra training tests required to join the elite counter-terrorism unit, yet young enough to withstand the body-punishing rigors of the job. The shooter's a man, it's safe to say, because there are no women in the SEALs. And there's a good chance he's white, though the SEALs have stepped up efforts to increase the number of minorities in their ranks... A 'positive thinker' who 'gets in trouble when he's not challenged' ... a man who 'flunked vacation and flunked relaxing.'" Whoever he is, the man is sitting on one hell of a secret, but it's part of the deal that they know they may never be publicly recognized for the work they do.

Escape from Abbottabad

THE MISSION'S CHIEF objective may have been met, but it wasn't over yet. Bin Laden was dead, but there was still the matter of combing the compound for every available piece of evidence they could take with them to illuminate his ongoing role in Al Qaeda and any imminent terrorist plots that may have been underway. All of this had to be achieved in just a few minutes, before any further resistance arrived. It is possible that the surgically-precise operation could have fallen foul of the Pakistani police or military, who were not fully aware of what was occurring and could easily have opened fire first and asked questions later.

The only person the SEALs took with them was bin Laden himself, at this stage no more than a six-foot-four dead weight. They had already photographed him *in situ* after the double tap that ended his life, but still needed to take the body for further identification and verification. In addition, they did not want to leave this powerful propaganda tool – the body of the man responsible for the most high-profile and deadly terrorist attacks against the West in the history of the world – in the hands of potential sympathizers.

As well as the body, the teams ransacked the compound for computer hard drives and other media that they could hand over to intelligence staff to piece together anything they could on bin Laden and Al Qaeda. Anyone they encountered who was not killed – predominantly women and children – were restrained with plastic handcuff strips and left behind for the Pakistani authorities to find.

With one stealth helicopter down, there was no way that both teams of SEALs could leave without help. By this stage, more than thirty minutes after they arrived at the compound, backup had arrived from the teams staged a ten-minute flight for just such an eventuality. Two Boeing Chinook helicopters would carry them to safety. Only one was strictly necessary, since they have plenty of capacity, but the experience with the Black Hawk required multiple redundancies. Temperatures were seventeen degrees hotter than expected, the chief factor that had led to the disastrous reduction in lift for the downed craft, and there might be no time to mount a second rescue.

But as the Chinooks approached to carry the first team to safety, there was the matter of the crashed Black Hawk to take care of first. An ordinary Black Hawk is a formidable helicopter, a tough and generally reliable craft with a range of three hundred sixty miles and all the tools and capabilities needed to contend in the harsh combat environment of the Middle East. But this one was something more, a highly classified stealth version that included military technology never seen before. The SEALs knew that they could not afford to allow it to fall into enemy hands, since its value to foreign military would be incalculable. The only option was to use an explosive charge to destroy as much of it as they could, hopefully rendering the sensitive instruments and other equipment useless. Otherwise, their success would come at a terrible price: the death of the terrorist chief in exchange for cutting-edge stealth technology that could put enemy forces years ahead of where they were and be used against the U.S.

The charge that ruined the flightless Black Hawk did not completely destroy it, and photographs of the wreckage soon appeared in media across the world, leading to endless speculation about its stealth modifications and their implications.

The *Mail* quoted Bill Sweetman, editor of *Aviation Week*, after he had seen a close-up photograph of the smashed rotor housing. "Well, now we know why all of us had trouble ID'ing the helicopter that crashed, or was brought down, in the Osama raid. It was a secretly developed stealth helicopter, probably a highly modified version of an H-60 Black Hawk. Photos show that the helicopter's tail features stealth-configured shapes on the boom and tip fairings, swept stabilizers and a 'dishpan' cover over a non-standard five-or-six-blade tail rotor." The level of detail and effort was in itself significant: this was a high-risk mission, but nevertheless one that military chiefs recognized required every piece of help they could offer – even if it meant potentially losing such valuable technology. "The willingness to compromise this technology shows the importance of the mission in the eyes of U.S. commanders – and what we're seeing here also explains why Pakistani defenses didn't see the first wave coming in. No wonder the team tried to destroy it." Other experts questioned whether what they were seeing was even a Black Hawk at all, certain key details of its appearance were so different from the standard craft.

One question the SEALs would ask themselves as they were carried away from the compound in Abbottabad over the mountainous Taliban territory back to their base in Afghanistan was, where would the wreckage of that downed helicopter end up? One of the best guesses is not that they would be used by the Pakistani military, or anywhere in the Middle East. Instead, suggested one former White House counterterrorism advisor, the most likely destination is China. "There are probably people in the Pentagon tonight who are very concerned that pieces of the helicopter may be, even now, on their way to China, because we know that China is trying to make stealth aircraft," said Richard Clarke. The Chinese and Pakistani military have a close relationship, and China has the technology and resources to make good use of the wreckage. It may well be that we will someday see the same modifications again, this time on a Chinese stealth helicopter. If so, that will be the price of doing business: it was a calculated risk, and one that the U.S. considered a cost worth paying for the death of Osama bin Laden.

Rising from the compound, the dust beneath the remaining Black Hawk and the two twin-rotor Chinooks swirling under the force of the downwash, the three aircraft were not out of danger yet. The insertion had gone quickly and covertly, but the plan relied on speed and they were now eight minutes behind schedule. As silent to radar and the ear as the Black Hawks were, as soon as the first had crashed and explosions started to occur they began attracting unwanted attention. Besides, the Chinooks were not as quiet, and by this point the Pakistani air force had spotted the unauthorized incursion into their airspace and was frantically scrambling fighter jets.

It seems that, as unaware as the Pakistani authorities were of the raid to begin with, there was no hope of escaping without serious risk of challenge, leading to engagement and unnecessary and politically catastrophic fatalities. At this point, it was deemed wise to inform the Pakistani intelligence services of what was going on. The jets converging on the site were recalled, and instead the police were left to clear up the mess left in the compound. When they finally arrived, they would find four corpses and a number of other people, trussed and ready for collection. Pakistani officials have said that there were around eighteen people there, although U.S. sources have claimed there were more than 20. Those picked up are said to include three of bin Laden's wives – including his youngest, Amal, who survived her leg wound – and 13 children, 11 of whom were boys. It is unknown how many of the children were bin Laden's own.

The work of the SEALs was over, but there was still much to be completed in the next 24 hours. The chief task was the identification and disposal of the body. Although there was little doubt in the minds of the U.S. authorities, the burden of proof was unusually high; there could be no room for doubt – although there will always be conspiracy theorists willing to suggest alternative scenarios.

The body was flown from the base in Bagram, Afghanistan to the Carl Vinson, an aircraft carrier then stationed in the North Arabian Sea. It was carried to its destination in a V-22 Osprey, a versatile military tiltrotor aircraft that combines the vertical take-off capabilities of a helicopter with the range and speed of a turboprop plane. Taking no chances of sabotage, the authorities had the V-22 escorted by two F/A-18s.

Identification of the body took many different forms and had taken place immediately after he was shot as well as on the Carl Vinson. For a start, there was simple visual identification. One of those said to have given a positive ID on the body was one of bin Laden's wives at the compound, back in Pakistan. It seems that another one of his wives had used his name to warn him of the approaching SEALs – thereby inadvertently giving away his identity. The body was measured and found to be 6 feet, 4 inches long, which matched the known height of bin Laden (in fact, one of the SEALs had lain beside the corpse and the height was estimated from a comparison, since they had no tape measure on hand). A photograph had also been sent to CIA specialists at Langley and was run through facial recognition software, producing a ninety to ninety-five percent match.

DNA testing was used to establish, beyond doubt, his connection to the bin Laden family. Osama bin Laden's sister had died some years earlier of brain cancer in Boston; the FBI had subpoenaed the body and taken samples of brain tissue and blood, storing them to create a DNA profile for future use. Their forethought proved invaluable at this point, since comparison with the samples taken from the body from Abbottabad proved beyond any reasonable doubt that it was her brother. Further tests were carried out with samples from his enormous extended family, and the chances of a false-positive were astronomically small.

Finally, there were the hard drives and other material removed from the compound. This transpired to include personal correspondence between bin Laden and other parties. Video footage confirmed that there could be only one identity for the owner. All the evidence pointed in the same direction: it had been bin Laden.

The identification was swift, but thorough. Despite the fact that he had been the most wanted man on the planet – and perhaps because of it – officials were keen to show all necessary respect and ensure that his burial conformed with Islamic law. The ethics of the means by which Osama bin Laden's location had been revealed were by no means clear cut and critics had already warned that the U.S. had lost their moral authority through the processes of torture and "aggressive interrogation." There was no need to add to the reasons for retaliation: this was one occasion on which they could show that they had played by the rules, and it cost them nothing.

U.S. officials have taken great pains to make it clear that the body was prepared for burial "in conformance with Islamic precepts and practice," as the White House's Press Secretary put it. Bin Laden's corpse was placed in a weighted bag and dropped from the side of the Carl Vinson into the Arabian Sea.

There were at least two major reasons for the sea burial. The first is that the U.S. would have been hard-pressed to find a country that would have been happy accepting the remains of the world's most notorious terrorist – and if they had, it would likely be a country with whom they would not do business. The second related reason is that a grave on land would immediately become a focus for jihadis, a shrine and a place to gather around. The anonymous and inaccessible grave at the bottom of the sea meant that this could never happen. But it also meant that no one would ever be able to verify bin Laden's death. The body had been disposed of and could never be recovered. A price worth paying, it was nevertheless one piece of information the conspiracy theorists would not forget.

There was one further question to decide with regards to the evidence, and that was how to go about convincing the public that bin Laden was, indeed, dead. Whether members of Al Qaeda, sympathizers in Afghanistan or Pakistan, or simply skeptical Americans, some sort of visible evidence that the man killed in the raid was bin Laden – rather than a look-alike, imposter or even U.S.-created fake – would be useful. In the hours that followed his sober but triumphant press conference, President Obama had to decide whether to release photographs of bin Laden's body or video footage of his burial. As with the burial, it was decided that anonymity and its attendant doubt were preferable to providing extremists with ammunition or inspiration. Photographs would be held back and not allowed to be left "floating around as incitement or propaganda tool."

THE WAR OF WORDS

THE DAYS AFTER the raid in Abbottabad were filled with a flurry of comment and activity among the press and on the Internet. This was landmark news, the end of an era, but quite possibly the beginning of a new period of uncertainty and danger. No one knew quite how this would impact Al Qaeda's strategy or motivation. In addition, there were many questions to answer about the manner in which the operation had been carried out, the judgment behind the calls that were made, and what it said about those who made them – chiefly President Barack Obama.

President Obama received a huge bump in approval ratings when news of bin Laden's death hit the airwaves. This was, finally, some degree of closure for the thousands of deaths on 9/11 that the previous administration – for all their efforts – had been unable to provide. Obama had achieved with intelligence, stealth and sheer *chutzpah* something that Bush had been unable to deliver with years of war and its resulting fallout.

Not only that, but the means by which he had ordered bin Laden's death was praised. He had not taken the easy option of an air strike, instead choosing the risky ground mission by SEALs – the only outcome that could provide sure evidence that their target was dead. Counterterrorism advisor John Brennan called it "one of the gutsiest calls of any president in recent memory," a sentiment that was probably correct and that was echoed the country over.

Struggling against popular opinion with a sluggish economic recovery and doubts about his grip on international affairs, the "Obama killed Osama" story pushed his approval ratings over the all-important fifty percent mark, up to fifty-six. (A month later it had slid back down into the '40s as concerns about the economy took hold again with a new wave of downbeat economic data.)

For all the fanfare, there were plenty who disagreed about both what had been achieved, and how. At home and abroad, critics suggested that bin Laden hadn't been "killed" – he had been assassinated or executed, without trial. The fact that he ostensibly hadn't been armed didn't help the case; at the time, it appears that he posed no immediate threat to the SEALs, who could therefore theoretically have arrested him and taken him away to face charges. This was swiftly countered by the administration by reports that he had been reaching for a nearby weapon – an AK-47 and a side-arm were reportedly present in the room where he was shot – and that it was reasonable for the SEALs to assume that anyone they encountered might have been wearing a suicide vest. The only safe and reasonable course of action, it was argued, was shooting first and worrying about the details later.

Nevertheless, there were still questions about the legality of the killing, particularly from human rights organizations, as well as many American journalists and commentators. Benjamin Ferencz – a specialist in international law who worked as a prosecutor in the Nuremburg trials – suggested that it would have been preferable to capture bin Laden and take him back to the U.S. or the Hague for judicial processing. "The issue here is whether what was done was an act of legitimate self-defense," he told the BBC World Service. "Killing a captive who poses no immediate threat is a crime under military law as well as all other law."

This point of view was swiftly addressed by U.S. Attorney General Eric Holder, who told the BBC that the mission was plainly lawful. It was, after all, a 'kill or capture' operation, meaning that – at least in theory – taking him alive had been an option. "If there was the possibility of a feasible surrender, that would have occurred," he said. Nevertheless, ensuring that the SEALs were safe took precedence over that objective, and killing him was quicker and easier than a potentially prolonged and messy capture operation. "One does not know what bin Laden had there. It's one o'clock, two o'clock in the morning or so, it's dark. This is a mass murderer who's sworn to continue his attacks against the United States and its allies. When confronted with that person, in the absence of some clear indication that he was going to surrender, I think that they acted in an appropriate way."

Of course, reason suggests that there was no outcome for Operation Neptune Spear that would have kept everyone happy. Perhaps in an ideal world, bin Laden would have been captured and taken back to the U.S. for trial. But how long would that take – and what would the punishment be? Where would he be kept, and would imprisoning him be an unacceptable risk for the safety of the country? Anywhere he was held would surely present a high-value target, both for Al Qaeda sympathizers and other Islamic extremists, but also for American vigilantes who wanted him dead and couldn't understand why it was taking so long to bring him to ultimate justice. And yet, the course that was taken meant that it appeared that the normal judicial processes had been circumvented: bin Laden had been assassinated, plain and simple, according to skeptics.

Legal experts started to comb through the details of the raid, many of which were constantly changing and evolving as new information came to light and things were clarified. To begin with, after all, there was no hope of a complete picture. Even Obama didn't know exactly what happened; the only ones who did were the SEALs who were present at the time, and they had acted quickly, instinctively, in darkness and under great pressure. The fragments would take a long time to piece together, and many details will no doubt remain classified for years to come.

The chief case for the critics' argument is that there was very little armed resistance. Only a few shots were fired by one man, at the very beginning of the raid – al-Kuwaiti, who was quickly killed. Other than that, no one in the compound was encountered who was carrying a gun. Bin Laden was not allowed a chance to surrender, whatever the slim chance that he would have done so. On the other hand, this could be considered part of the ongoing battle against Al Qaeda. U.S. Attorney General Eric Holder stated that, rather than an assassination, this was "an act of national self-defense" against the Al Qaeda leader who had openly admitted his role in planning 9/11. "You have to remember, it is lawful to target an enemy commander," he said. International law allows for the targeting of enemy commanders. "I actually think that the dotting of the i's and the crossing of the t's is what separates the United States, the United Kingdom, our allies, from those who we are fighting," he added. "We do respect the rule of law, there are appropriate ways in which we conduct ourselves and expect our people to conduct themselves, and I think those Navy SEALs conducted themselves in a way that's consistent with American and British values." Philip Bobbitt, a specialist on constitutional law and international security, told the BBC, "I don't think that this is an extrajudicial killing ... I think this is part of an armed conflict authorized by the United Nations, authorized by both houses of Congress."

This is a debate that will no doubt run for years, but the fact remains: bin Laden is dead, killed by well-trained SEALs executing a carefully planned mission that had been ten years in the making and played extremely well with the majority of the U.S. population – those people living regular lives, with no interest or training in constitutional law, whose lives had been turned upside-down by the terrorist attacks that killed their friends and relatives and threatened the safety and stability of their country.

Further criticism would come from some Islamic experts, who took exception to the way that bin Laden's body was handled. Although the U.S. had done everything it thought necessary to conform with Islamic law – washing, shrouding and burying the body within twenty-four hours – some experts disagreed. Generally, bodies are supposed to be buried with the head pointing towards the holy city of Mecca. Islamic tradition does allow for burial at sea, but only in exceptional circumstances. Burial at sea is allowed if the person was at sea at the time and a long voyage to reach land might lead to advanced decomposition. If there is a risk that the grave would be desecrated or dug up, this is also a case in favor of a sea burial. In these instances, the body should be protected from being eaten by the fish, perhaps by being encased in a clay shell. The *Guardian* quoted a number of experts in the field. "Mohammed al-Qubaisi, Dubai's grand mufti, said of bin Laden's burial: 'They can say they buried him at sea, but they cannot say they did it according to Islam. Sea burials are permissible for Muslims in extraordinary circumstances. This is not one of them.' Abdul-Sattar al-Janabi, who preaches at Baghdad's Abu Hanifa mosque, said: 'What was done by the Americans is forbidden by Islam and might provoke some Muslims. It is not acceptable and it is almost a crime to throw the body of a Muslim man into the sea. The body of bin Laden should have been handed over to his family to look for a country to bury him. 'The radical Lebanon-based cleric Omar Bakri Mohammed said: 'The Americans want to humiliate Muslims through this burial, and I don't think this is in the interest of the U.S. administration.' "

Fortunately, far more serious than any problems it would cause for the image of the U.S. were the effects on Al Qaeda itself. The organization – really a loose affiliation of terrorist cells and movements, rather than a well-structured group – had already been badly undermined by the killing of its figurehead. To begin with, in the first hours after the news was announced, it was believed that this was all bin Laden was – a figurehead. A figure of inspiration to jihadis and terrorists, perhaps, but someone who had been on the run and in hiding since 2001 and who had not had any active part in planning new terrorist activities for years.

This quickly changed with the analysis of the flash drives and computer equipment recovered from the compound, along with other evidence. In fact, experts concluded, bin Laden had been closely involved in the running of Al Qaeda and the planning of new atrocities. Killing him had not only been an ideological blow to world terrorism: it had been an important practical step in undermining further ongoing plots.

Barack Obama refused to release photographs of bin Laden's corpse, on the grounds that they could be used as powerful propaganda and recruiting tools by Al Qaeda. A smarter move was the release of video footage of him recovered by the SEALs. If he was the Al Qaeda mastermind, this material presented a very different impression of him than the charismatic jihadi who inspired so many followers.

The videos released show a tall, thin man sitting hunched on the floor, wrapped in a dirty-looking blanket. He holds a remote control in his hand, pointed at the TV on which he views images of himself. He strokes his greying beard, rocking gently back and furth in the dingy squalor of his surroundings. The intended message is clear: here is the great man, reduced in his self-imposed captivity to reliving his glory days in the only way available to him: news footage played on a small, portable TV. The Pentagon had huge amounts of material at its disposal, and yet a few short clips were all they released. This was indeed a war of propaganda, but other clips give a rather different impression from the burned out shell of a man the first presented: bin Laden, animated and focused, delivering more of the charismatic video messages that proclaim his ideology and incite others to join the cause – still a force to be reckoned with.

One of the stranger, and unverified statements to emerge about the videos found in the compound was that they included a number of pornographic films – something strongly forbidden by Islam. If this information can be taken seriously, then it's still unclear who they belonged to, or who viewed them. Nevertheless, if true, then it represents a significant blow to the image of the icon of faith that bin Laden had become to some Muslims.

These were only a small selection of the images, videos and texts found in Abbottabad – what the Pentagon called "the largest collection of terrorist material ever." Amongst other things, the cache established beyond doubt the role that he played in different Al Qaeda operations in the Middle East – including in the Yemen-based "Al Qaeda in the Arabian Peninsula" group. It is also hoped that the evidence will enable the capture or killing of other key figures who still remain at large. A few days after the raid on bin Laden's compound, a U.S. drone strike was launched against a remote corner of Yemen, thought to be the location in which Anwar al-Awlaki was hiding. Al-Awlaki, a dual U.S. and Yemeni citizen, is a former imam and lecturer on Islam whose words have inspired and guided many high-profile terrorists – including three of the 9/11 hijackers and the Times Square bomber. He now appears to have a far more active role in Al Qaeda, to the point where the Pentagon has described him as "more dangerous than even bin Laden." Al-Awlaki was not harmed in the strike, which killed only two militants of low rank. Nevertheless, the timing raises interesting questions as to whether the U.S. were acting quickly on information they had acquired through the raid just a few days earlier.

Then, of course, there was the reaction by Al Qaeda itself. Al Qaeda does not have a unified voice and is not a homogeneous, top-down-led organization. Therefore it is often difficult to know how much one comment reflects the mood of the rest. However, the killing of their spiritual and literal leader, by an unauthorized U.S. mission on Pakistani soil and ending with the hasty and illegitimate burial of bin Laden, was something they could gather around. The U.S. knew this was always going to be a danger, but it was the price of taking down the world's most wanted and dangerous terrorist. Condemnation and the threat of retribution came quickly from Al Qaeda, in the form of a statement on many different well-known jihadi websites. The statement acknowledged that Osama bin Laden had, indeed, been killed – an admission that was by no means expected. The swift disposal of the body and secrecy around the photographs of the corpse could have been used against the U.S., with Al Qaeda denying that bin Laden had been shot. However, the spokesman wrote that their leader had been murdered, and vowed vengeance on behalf of the *Ummah* – the worldwide community of Muslims.

"On an historical day of the days of the great Islamic Ummah... the mujahid migrant ascetic leader – Sheikh Abu Abdullah Osama bin Mohammed bin Laden (may God bless his soul) has been killed in a moment of truthfulness, for he made his word truthful to his actions... He refused to accept vice in exchange for his religion, or to submit and be humiliated by the misguided and the receivers of the wrath of God, who have been stricken by disgrace and misery. The sheikh faced the weapon with weapon, force with force, and accepted to challenge the supercilious throngs that came out arrogantly and ostentatiously with their machinery, gear, aircrafts, and armies."

Rewriting history, the eulogy claimed that bin Laden had met the SEALs nobly, with brave, armed resistance before his death. "Despite all this, his determination never wavered and his strength was never weakened; he instead stood up to them, face-to-face like a high mountain. He continued to fight the kind of battles that he was accustomed to... until he received the bullets of deception and non-belief to surrender his soul to its Creator."

Finally, there was the unavoidable call to action. "We in Al Qaeda vow to God the Exalted and seek His support to help us go forward on the path of jihad that was trekked by our leaders, headed by Sheikh Osama ... We will not relent or hesitate; we will not stray or quit until God judges between us and our enemies by the truth, He indeed is the fairest of judges. We stress that Sheikh Osama's blood, God bless his soul, is more precious to us and to every Muslim to go in vain. It will, God willing, remain a curse that will chase and haunt the Americans and their agents inside and outside the country. Very soon, God willing, their joy will turn into mourning and their blood will be mixed with their tears. We will fulfill Sheikh Osama's oath, God bless his soul: 'America and anyone who lives in America will not enjoy peace until our people in Palestine enjoy it.'"

"The soldiers of Islam, whether in groups or individually, will not relent, despair, surrender, or weaken and will continue to plan until you are afflicted with a catastrophe that turns your children's hair grey prematurely ... We call on our Muslim people in Pakistan where Sheikh Osama was killed to revolt and wash this shame brought upon them by a band of traitors and bandits who sold out to the Ummah's enemies and disparaged the sentiment of this noble, mujahid people. We call on them to revolt altogether to cleanse their country, Pakistan, of the American filth who spread mischief in the land. The sheikh refused to depart this life before sharing his Muslim Ummah its happiness with the revolutions against injustice and wrongdoers. He, may God bless his soul, recorded a message one week before he died, which included a congratulatory note, advice, and guidance that will soon, God willing, be disseminated. He concluded his message with these poetic verses: 'Telling the tyrant the truth is the honor and the hope. It is the path to this life and the path to the next. You can choose to die a slave or a freeborn.'"

Al Qaeda's leadership had thrown down the gauntlet to its members, as well as to every Islamic extremist on the planet and every Pakistani Muslim incensed by American interference.

A postscript to bin Laden's ignominious end in that compound in Abbottabad comes in the form of a series of documents that came to light courtesy of whistle-blowing website WikiLeaks, detailing the contents of a long line of arrests, medical records and interrogations of the seven hundred eighty detainees who have ever been brought to the notorious Guantanamo Bay prison in Cuba. One of these detainees was the infamous and extremely dangerous 9/11-mastermind planner, Khalid Sheikh Mohammed.

The timing was apt: only a week before the raid occurred, the leaked documents hit the headlines. In a seemingly prophetic statement, KSM had warned what would happen if coalition forces captured or killed the Al Qaeda leader. His organization would detonate a stolen weapon of mass destruction on a European target, unleashing what he promised would be a "nuclear hellstorm."

There is no way of knowing whether KSM's threat was an empty one, an unreliable boast extracted under the torture of the one hundred eighty-three times he was waterboarded – or whether it reflects some kind of reality. It seems unlikely that Al Qaeda would have managed to acquire a nuclear weapon without alerting the authorities, or that they would have held onto it for so long, risking discovery and the loss of such a potent tool in their struggle. But equally, bin Laden's killing by U.S. forces was a significant goad to worldwide Islamic extremism, laying down an immediate challenge to Al Qaeda to answer such a high-profile humiliation. And no one really knew what effect the death would have on the structure of that elusive and shadowy organization. The question in the minds of many counterterrorism officials must have been: Was it cutting the head off a snake, or the head off a hydra?

BIRTH OF A TERRORIST

THE METEORIC RISE OF
SHEIKH BIN LADEN

THE NAME OSAMA MEANS "young lion..." Often a name will reflect parents hopes for the kind of person their child will grow into. Perhaps this was the case with bin Laden, but it seems unlikely that his father would have taken this attention to detail with all of his sons and daughters. There is no universally accepted family tree for the complex and sprawling bin Laden family, but it is generally believed that his father, Mohammed bin Laden, fathered something like fifty-eight children.

Osama bin Mohammed bin Awad bin Laden, to give him his full name, was born in 1957, in Riyadh, the capital of Saudi Arabia. Information about the precise date of his birth is also sketchy, but in one interview in 1998 that was later broadcast by Al Jazeera, he stated that his birthday was March 10.

The young Osama was born into a wealthy, if somewhat fragmented family. In total, the patriarch of the bin Laden family is said to have had twenty-two wives. However, in observance with Sharia law, he ensured that he was only married to four at any given time. As his wives aged he would divorce them and marry younger women. Osama was, by the best estimate, his father's seventeenth child – although it is worth noting that he was the only child by that mother, his tenth wife, a Syrian-born woman called Hamida al-Attas.

Sheikh Mohammed bin Awad bin Laden was by all accounts a formidable businessman. He was an extremely successful, wealthy and well-connected man who had worked his way up from literally nothing to being a confidante and associate of the Saudi royal family. The title "Sheikh" can mean a number of things in Arabic, but it is broadly an honorific meaning "elder," often used to designate an Islamic scholar, the elder of a tribe or an otherwise revered wise man. It had been a long way for the wealthy Mohammed to climb from his poverty-stricken origins.

Born in Yemen in 1908, Mohammed had emigrated to Saudi Arabia when he was still a young boy. Accounts vary, but it appears that he had been an uneducated and poor farmer's son from the Hadramaut – an inhospitable region of Yemen in the southern part of the Arabian Peninsula. The name "Hadramaut" means "death is among us," although whether it was named for the short life-expectancies of its poor inhabitants or the frequent and bloody battles that had been fought there in certain periods of history is unclear.

Either way, Mohammed hadn't wanted to stay around to find out. At the age of forteen he had taken passage on an overcrowded *dhow*, a traditional Arab sailing boat, north across the Red Sea. He somehow made his way, tired and hungry, across the desert to Jeddah. Now, Jeddah is one of the major cities of Saudi Arabia and the gateway to the holy city of Mecca. At the time, however, it was a small, poor place.

Mohammed had risked his life to escape Yemen and find his fortune, and he didn't give up. He began working as a porter in Jeddah. Where others saw misery and poverty, he saw potential and opportunity. He had ambition and determination, but he also had inspiration. Mohammed had come from the Hadramaut, where he had witnessed the construction of the tall clay-brick towers in which many of his countrymen lived. He knew that there was an opportunity in Jeddah to build the same, replacing the space-inefficient houses he saw around him there.

But starting his own company would take money, and he didn't have that. To build the necessary capital he worked like a fiend, saving everything he could. He took a number of jobs – working in a shop for pilgrims, cooking, quarrying and others – and slept on the bare sand to avoid unnecessary expense. In the early 1930s, he had enough to begin his own building firm. He started with the high-rises of his childhood memories and swiftly progressed and diversified into dams and roads. It was the days of the first oil boom, and before long he came to the attention of the increasingly prosperous Saudi royal family. To begin with, he forged a strong working relationship with Abdul Aziz Ibn Saud, the country's first monarch and the founder and unifier of Saudi Arabia. He would stay loyal to the family and made it his mission to be unfailingly reliable. He would also make a point of offering the lowest price for construction work, winning him contract after contract. As a result of his connections and reputation, the bin Laden family would eventually become known as the "wealthiest non-royal family in the kingdom." In some cases, where it was a religious matter or might ingratiate him with the authorities – the two are hard to separate in such a culture – he would complete projects at cost. Biographer Peter Bergen relates how Osama bin Laden himself spoke of his father's business sense and religious sensibilities to Al Jazeera in 1998. "God blessed him and bestowed on him an honor that no other building contractor has known. He built the holy Mecca mosque and at the same time – because of God's blessings to him – he built the holy mosque in Medina. When he found out that the government of Jordan announced a tender for restoration work on the Dome of the Rock Mosque [in Jerusalem], he gathered engineers and asked them, 'Calculate only the cost price of the project.' He was awarded the project."

But Mohammed bin Laden wasn't just a shrewd businessman. He was a shrewd politician, too. After Abdul Aziz died in 1953, there was a struggle for power between his two eldest sons, Faisal and Saud. Mohammed bin Laden became close to Prince Faisal, the half-brother of King Saud, who succeeded Abdul Aziz. The Saud era had been tremendously wasteful and almost ruinous to the economy; despite climbing oil prices, the kingdom was insolvent. In 1964 Faisal deposed his half-brother and took the throne. He set about rebuilding the economy, helped by none other than Mohammed bin Laden. As a reward for his financial assistance, the newly crowned King Faisal issued a royal decree: all future state construction projects would be awarded to the bin Laden company. Mohammed bin Laden was now effectively responsible for the entire physical infrastructure of Saudi Arabia, and his fortune grew to the empire that is now worth five billion dollars. After his death in 1967 the business was taken over by his oldest son, Salem, but all of the family received a slice of the wealth.

Unlike the Sauds, Mohammed bin Laden did not let his growing wealth go to his head. He had been born in abject poverty and had worked hard for what he had. In contrast to many other rich Saudis, he lived a simple life and maintained a devout faith – insisting that his many children did the same. Nevertheless, the reasons for his son's fanaticism do not lie with Mohammed bin Laden. In fact, the family is a mess of contradictions, with different sons encompassing wildly different approaches to the West. Pulitzer Prize-winning journalist Steve Coll has become an authority on the bin Laden family after writing his book, *The bin Ladens: An Arabian Family in the American Century*. In an interview with the German newspaper *Spiegel*, he stated that "the bin Ladens have always been a clan that encompasses an astonishingly broad range of ideologies – from those of its completely worldly members, like *bon vivant* Salem bin Laden, a Beatles fan and playboy, to those of its religious fanatics. This diversity was also evident on that fateful day in America. When the terrorists slammed their hijacked American Airlines jet into the Pentagon, Shafiq bin Laden, Osama's half-brother, was in a conference with investors at the Ritz Carlton Hotel in Washington, just a few miles away. The conference was sponsored by the Carlyle Group, in which both the bin Ladens and the Bush family held shares." That link between the bin Ladens and the Bush family would later be probed in depth as a country asking itself how this could happen turned its anguish in every direction.

Mohammed bin Laden was devout, but he was also a modernizer and a cosmopolitan man. For example, he would employ Christians and other non-Muslims on the construction site in Jerusalem, where he was renovating the Al-Aqsa Mosque – Islam's third holiest site, located on Temple Mount. In addition, Coll says that he "bought more than half a dozen modern Packard two-seaters from the United States and was the first private citizen in Saudi Arabia to have his own airplane." This was not a man to turn his back on opportunity or technology simply because it did not have Islamic origins. Osama bin Laden, by his early twenties, would start doing exactly that.

For all his religious and moral strictness, Osama's father had a curious idea of family. Although Osama was heir to part of Mohammed's enormous fortune, he did not have much to do with the man. His parents divorced not long after Osama was born, and he did not live with his father after that. Instead, his mother remarried – a man called Muhammed al-Attas, an employee of the bin Laden company. They had four children together, and Osama lived with his mother, step-father, three step-brothers and one step-sister in their new house.

Little is known about Osama bin Laden's elementary education, although we do know that his father made sure he was going to school. Coll observes that Osama appears to have attended schools that were "influenced by Western curricula and culture." Although he would have studied the Qur'an, like many Saudi boys, he did not attend a *madrassa* – one of the religious schools that have come in for criticism in recent years for their focus on indoctrinating religious education at the expense of other areas of study. It is likely that the new family lived in Syria

– his mother's country of birth – for some time, where Osama was also educated.

Returning to Jeddah, Osama was sent to the Al-Thager Model School. To begin with, in the 1960s, it was comparatively secular in character, though this would soon change. Roughly translated as "the Haven," the school had been built by King Faisal and became known as a prestigious destination for the sons of rich businessmen and royals. Bin Laden was, according to Coll, "a solid if unspectacular student" – certainly not the top of his class. Bergen records the opinion of Brian Fyfield-Shayler, a Brit living in Saudi Arabia at the time who taught English to several of the bin Laden sons, including Osama, who arrived in his classroom in 1968. "All the sons are very good-looking. I don't think that I have ever met any ugly bin Ladens. Osama's mother, I am told, was a great beauty. Since his father never had more than four wives at any given time, he was constantly divorcing the third and the fourth and taking in new ones. This was an anachronism even in the 1950s and 60s. This was my fourth year teaching, when Osama came along. Osama was one of 30 students. He used to sit two-thirds of the way back on the window side that looked out onto sports fields and playing grounds. Why did I remember Osama? First of all, I would have noticed because of his name, because of the family, and, of course, when you walked into a class of anyone of his age, he was literally outstanding, because he was taller than his contemporaries, and so he was very noticeable. His English was not amazing. He was not one of the great brains of that class."

Osama was raised as a Wahhabi, the branch of Islam that is the most dominant in Saudi Arabia. Its founder was an eighteenth-century theologian called Muhammad Ibn Abd al-Wahhab, one of whose tenets was the purging of Islam from what he considered impurities. Much ink has been spilt on the connection between Wahhabism and Osama bin Laden's militant jihadi ideology. To blame his terrorism on this form of Islam is doubtless simplistic.

Although it might be fair to state that it formed the foundations of his faith, there were many later influences that came to bear on him, especially at university. One expert, Natana De Long-Bas at Georgetown University, argues, "The militant Islam of Osama bin Laden did not have its origins in the teachings of Ibn Abd-al-Wahhab and was not representative of Wahhabi Islam as it is practiced in contemporary Saudi Arabia, yet for the media it came to define Wahhabi Islam during the later years of bin Laden's lifetime. However 'unrepresentative' bin Laden's global jihad was of Islam in general and Wahhabi Islam in particular, its prominence in headline news took Wahhabi Islam across the spectrum from revival and reform to global jihad."

Other experts have drawn a distinction between the highly conservative form of Islam represented by Wahhabism and the militant, political Islam that has arisen in recent years. It may be true that Saudi Wahhabis have funded fundamentalist Muslim groups, including the Muslim Brotherhood, but at the same time they opposed jihadi resistance against Muslim leaders.

Writing in the UK's *Guardian*, comparative religion commentator Karen Armstrong states, "The Qur'an prohibits aggressive warfare, permits war only in self-defense and insists that the true Islamic values are peace, reconciliation and forgiveness. It also states firmly that there must be no coercion in religious matters, and for centuries Islam had a much better record of religious tolerance than Christianity.

"Like the Bible, the Qur'an has its share of aggressive texts, but like all the great religions, its main thrust is toward kindliness and compassion. Islamic law outlaws war against any country in which Muslims are allowed to practice their religion freely, and forbids the use of fire, the destruction of buildings and the killing of innocent civilians in a military campaign. So although Muslims, like Christians or Jews, have all too often failed to live up to their ideals, it is not because of the religion per se.

"At our conference in Washington, many people favored 'Wahhabi terrorism.' They pointed out that most of the hijackers on September 11 came from Saudi Arabia, where a peculiarly intolerant form of Islam known as Wahhabism was the state religion. They argued that this description would be popular with those many Muslims who tended to be hostile to the Saudis. I was not happy, however, because even though the narrow, sometimes bigoted vision of Wahhabism makes it a fruitful ground for extremism, the vast majority of Wahhabis do not commit acts of terror."

Although the young bin Laden's parents had divorced early on in his life, his father still loomed large and took a personal interest in both his school education and religious identity. The visits were only occasional, but memorable. He would take Osama on pilgrimages to Mecca and Medina – the first and second holiest cities in Islam – in both of which Mohammed's company had carried out renovation work. Bergen quotes Jamal Khalifa, bin Laden's brother-in-law, on the relationship between father and son: "He liked his father very much. He considered him as a model. He was not with his father much, because his father died when he was ten years old. And, also, the father didn't meet his children much. He was very busy – a lot of children, a lot of houses – so he just met them officially. There are fifty-four children, and he had twenty-plus wives."

Neither Mohammed nor traditional Wahhabism can be blamed for turning Osama into a terrorist, but what is likely is that a vacuum was created by his father's death, leaving the way open for more radical influences in the young boy's life

THE GAP OPENS

OSAMA WAS ONLY TEN years old when his father died, the victim of a plane crash in September 1967. A progressive man, Mohammed bin Laden had been the first Saudi to own a private airplane. His pilot on that day had been an American.

Although Osama was his seventeenth of a total of more than fifty children, Mohammed had loomed large in his life. The death made him a wealthy child. The male heirs inherited a 2.3 percent share in the massive construction and oil empire, with each of the daughters seeing less than half of that, one percent. His oldest son, Salem bin Laden, would later take charge of the business. "He was," writes bin Laden expert Steve Coll, "at least ten years older than his brother Osama and had attended a British boarding school." The school in question was Millfield, a private school in Somerset in the southwest of England. This is probably the place where Salem learned to love the Beatles, whose songs he would play on his guitar.

Islamic law forbids the charging of interest, in much the same way that the Israelite economic laws of the Old Testament do. In Islamic finance this is still strictly observed today (meaning that there are financial instruments and work-arounds that are not common in the West). Nevertheless, the money that Osama received, along with the profits his share of the company earned, were invested in western banks, earning interest and growing every year. Some people have claimed that, as a result, bin

Laden was at one point worth somewhere in the region of three hundred million dollars, although others have suggested this is an exaggeration. The reality is probably an order of magnitude less, though still a substantial sum.

One has to wonder what Osama made of the tension between traditional Islamic values and the Western influence to which he was subjected. His father's openness to progress and Western ideas had led to his death, and then helped to make his son rich. His school, too – the Al-Thager Model School – was another example of that curious contradiction. It was a modern, comparatively secular school and the best in the region. Its subjects included English language, taught by men who had come from the UK, and the pupils had to wear uniforms like those required in British prep schools. In contrast to the traditional ankle-length shirts or *thobes* worn in other Saudi schools, Osama had to don a shirt and tie, trousers and a blazer.

One of Bergen's stories from this time demonstrates how the young Osama bin Laden appeared to have a surprisingly westernized, consumeristic view of the world as a young teenager – in contrast to the extremism-driven passion for austerity that characterized his later years. In 1970 Salem bin Laden took his younger brother with him to a town in Sweden called Falun, where they stayed at the expensive Hotel Astoria. The manager related how the wealthy young brothers had shown a carelessly dismissive attitude towards their newly-found money, and the privileges that came with it. "They came with a big Rolls-Royce, and it was forbidden to park the car outside the building in this street. But they did it, and we said to them, 'You have to pay a fine for every day and every hour you are staying outside this hotel,' but they said, 'Oh, it doesn't matter – it's so funny to go to the police station and to talk with the police. We will stay where we are.' It was like a joke to them. They had so much money they didn't know how much money they had ... I asked them how they had managed to come to Sweden with this enormous Rolls-Royce. They said, 'We have our plane.'

"They stayed one week ... They were dressed very exclusive ... They had two double rooms. They slept in one bed and on the other bed they had their bags. On Sunday, I had no cleaner at the hotel, so I took care of the room myself, and I was shocked because in the big bag they had lots of white, expensive shirts from Dior and Yves Saint Laurent. When they had worn the shirt once, they dropped it. So the cleaner had taken these shirts to wash them, but they said, 'No, we are just using them once, so you can have them if you want.'"

No doubt this was not the attitude that Mohammed bin Laden had hoped to inspire in his sons when he sent them to the Al-Thager Model School in Jeddah. Despite its Western influence, the school also placed a strong emphasis on religion, as might be expected. Pupils were expected to pray at noontime, as required by Islamic law. Discipline was strict. Every morning they would line up in rows for roll call, like soldiers on parade. Misdemeanors were punished by hitting the boys on the feet with a cane. Perhaps Osama came to associate the Western influence with this corporal punishment, or perhaps he already saw it as un-Islamic.

A balancing force for this nascent Westernization would come in the form of the Muslim Brotherhood. During the 1960s, King Faisal had welcomed teachers from Egypt and Syria who had been expelled from their own countries for their involvement in extremism and dissident organizations. Many of these ended up teaching in the Saudi education system, including at Al-Thager. Their influence on the young bin Laden is clear; he became a member of the Muslim Brotherhood and started going to study groups after school to learn more about its political ideas.

The Muslim Brotherhood, often known as MB or simply the Brotherhood has been called the world's most influential Islamist movement. It is one of the largest and oldest Muslim organizations, tracing its origins back to Hassan al-Banna, an

Islamic scholar and schoolteacher, in 1928. The Brotherhood now comprises a significant proportion of political opposition in many Arab states – seen recently in Egypt, a country from which they have repeatedly been banned for trying to overthrow the secular government. (In the event, popular uprising achieved what extremism could not.)

Under the slogan "Islam is the answer," the MB aims to promote Islam as the only framework for ordering the lives of Muslim individuals, organizations and states. This uncompromising attitude has led to a broad range of interpretations, both within and outside the movement. There is also disagreement on the level of violence supported by the Brotherhood, although this likely varies widely. Officially, the MB does not condone any use of violence in furthering its ends, and has not for some decades. Nevertheless, in the past, it has been associated with more violent methods, hence the ongoing skepticism from some quarters.

9/11 was a watershed for many Islamic organizations as well as many Western groups. The terrorist attacks demanded a response, and no one could sit on the fence – extremism could no longer be considered a form of harmless eccentricity. The Muslim Brotherhood published a statement, signed by over 40 prominent Muslim scholars and politicians, stating categorically that they did not agree with these extremists and condemned their actions. "The undersigned, leaders of Islamic movements, are horrified by the events of Tuesday, September 11, 2001 in the United States which resulted in massive killing, destruction and attack on innocent lives. We express our deepest sympathies and sorrow. We condemn, in the strongest terms, the incidents, which are against all human and Islamic norms. This is grounded in the Noble Laws of Islam which forbid all forms of attacks on innocents. God Almighty says in the Holy Qur'an: 'No bearer of burdens can bear the burden of another' (Surah al-Isra 17:15)."

Over a year before bin Laden's death at the hands of the SEALs in his compound in Abbottabad, elements within the Brotherhood were not only condemning Al Qaeda but even questioning its relevance. Writing for the *Huffington Post* and taken up on the English site of the MB, Shadi Hamid suggested, "Al Qaeda is spent as an ideological force in the Arab and Muslim world, so we might as well come out and say it, and, hopefully, act like it too. It's not so much that Al Qaeda is irrelevant – it isn't – but, rather, that it is, and has increasingly become, beside the point. Having lived in Jordan in 2008 and now in Doha, it's really quite remarkable the extent to which Al Qaeda doesn't figure into Arab conversations about the future of the Arab world. Except it's not remarkable. Al Qaeda never intended to win the hearts and minds of Muslims and become what might be called a membership organization. In fact, it preferred less, rather than more, active supporters. There have generally been two predominant models of Islamist activism – one of bottom-up society and institution-building, exemplified by the Muslim Brotherhood, and another that focuses on top-down seizure of power, through a mobilized, ideologically-committed vanguard. Al Qaeda and its offshoots have always been of the latter category. Its model is simple – to use small numbers for big effect, and, in this, there is little doubt they succeeded, at least for a time."

So, bin Laden's approach to political chance would diverge from the Muslim Brotherhood's in his later years, but as a child he was deeply committed to the cause. Some years ago Edouard Ahajot-Artzrunik spoke to Top Spot about a chance meeting he had once had with the bin Laden family. At the time, Ed was in partnership with a prominent Saudi and in the construction business. More specifically, he took part in building a major road to Mecca. Given their contracts for Saudi infrastructure, it was only natural that Ed should come across the bin Ladens – or, at least, some of them, including the young Osama. He remembers Osama as a quiet, but very intelligent boy, and drawn to radical ideas even then. Ed has since died but – tempering Coll's assertion that he was only a mediocre student – he recalled a child who read prodigiously and was clearly a thinker.

Neither Osama bin Laden's family nor his schooling can explain his lurch towards violent extremism, though. There is no doubt that he was a devout Muslim from a young age; there are certain things that he did to replicate the actions of the Prophet Mohammed in his own life – such as eating with the fingers of his right hand, rather than with a spoon, as well as fasting, dressing and sitting in the ways that he understood the Prophet did – that suggests a tremendous respect. He was known as an ascetic man, despite his huge wealth. In the book *Looming Tower*, the author Lawrence Wright describes how, when he was living in Sudan, bin Laden would have a lamb killed and cooked every day for his guests. He, though, "ate very little himself, preferring to nibble what his guests left on their plates, believing that these abandoned morsels would gain the favor of God." So, his childhood laid the foundations, but it was his time at university that made Osama bin Laden the man who would kill and injure thousands of people in his own personal holy war.

With his oldest brother overseeing the family business, it was not until he was seventeen that he took a personal interest in the construction empire. This age seems to mark the point at which he became an adult: as well as taking a more active role in the corporation and attending university to study civil engineering – clearly useful to a man who was heir to a share of billions of dollars worth of construction revenue – he also got married.

Ever since his parents had divorced, Osama had accompanied his mother on regular trips back to her home country of Syria to see her family. During these visits he came to know Najwa Ghanem, his first cousin – her father is Osama's mother's brother – who was three years younger than him. She belonged to a farming community, as her parents still do; the Syrian side of his family benefited nothing from the bin Ladens' millions.

A marriage between the two of them was arranged, and in 1974 he traveled to Latakia, Syria's main port city, to collect her and take her back to Saudi. She was fourteen at the time. Over the course of the next twenty-five or so years, Osama would marry another four women – though, like his father, he did not break Islamic law by having more than four wives at one time. In contrast to his father's approach to polygamy, he made a point of doing it in what he considered the "right" way. In his book *The Osama bin Laden I Know*, Peter Bergen recalls how Osama's friend and brother-in-law talked over the subject with him, determining that polygamy served a valuable social purpose but should not be abused, in the way that their fathers had both exploited the loopholes it presented. "We discussed polygamy, and we recalled how our fathers practiced polygamy. We found that they were practicing it in a wrong way, where they are married and divorced, married and divorced – a lot of wives ... Some of those practicing polygamy will, if they marry the second one, neglect the first one. That's not the Islamic way at all ... And we look at polygamy as solving a social problem, especially when it's confirmed that there are more women than men in the society ... It's not fun, it's not a matter of just having women with you to sleep with – it's a solution for a problem. So that's how we looked at it, and we decided to practice it and to be a model."

As the first of his five wives, Osama moved Najwa in with him and his mother until after their first child was born in 1978. She would bear him at least another ten children until the two of them divorced – in 2001, not only when the 9/11 attacks brought new pressure to bear on him, but also when he married his most recent wife, Amal al-Sadah. The youngest and least educated of his wives, Najwa has been described by her sister-in-law, Carmen bin Laden, as "meek, submissive, highly religious and constantly pregnant."

It is through Najwa and one of their sons, Omar, that some of the most interesting insights about Osama bin Laden have come. The two of them, along with help from an American writer have authored the book, *Growing Up bin Laden*. This paints a picture of Osama as a father who is simultaneously harsh and uninvolved, at least emotionally: a disciplinarian who cared more about raising disciples than about the demands of fatherhood.

Najwa recalls some of the curious eccentricities of her husband – oddities that were seemingly sparked only because he considered them un-Islamic. He would forbid them to use air conditioning or refrigerators, even in the desert heat. The use of straws and drinking directly from the bottle were also not allowed. Throughout the hardships of life on the move, since bin Laden became *persona non grata* in Saudi Arabia and Sudan, his son yearns to know his father and cannot believe the stories about him – until he finally sees the video messages after 9/11 and can no longer deny it.

Time magazine summarizes, "Omar's early childhood is both charmed and abusive. Though the family inhabited a mansion in the Saudi city of Jeddah and owned horse ranches in the desert, their father refused to let them have toys, take modern medicine or use almost any modern conveniences except for lightbulbs, automobiles and firearms. Though Osama would punish his boys for laughing or smiling and send them on forced marches in the desert without water, Omar and his brothers could at least console themselves with the honor of being sons of the man who helped defeat the Soviet Union in Afghanistan, a hero in both the Muslim world and the West. 'When I was a young boy, I worshipped my father, whom I believed to be not only the most brilliant, but also the tallest man in the world,' Omar writes. 'I would have to go to Afghanistan to meet a man taller than my father. In truth, I would have to go to Afghanistan to truly come to know my father.'"

But fatherhood and jihad were still some years away. Osama first attended King Abdulaziz University in Jeddah, where he studied civil engineering. (Some sources have claimed that he also received an offer to the prestigious Oxford University in the UK, but turned it down to pursue his interests in the Muslim Brotherhood.) His religious horizons were broadened when he encountered the work of Sayyid Qutb, the author of *Milestones* – a call to action to recreate Islam around solely Qur'anic principles. Sayyid Qutb had been hanged in 1966, along with six other members of the Muslim Brotherhood, for plotting to overthrow the Egyptian state. His brother, Muhammad Qutb, was a lecturer at the university that bin Laden attended and an enthusiastic promoter of Sayyid's work. In one videotaped message from October 2003, bin Laden offers a rare reading list of three books to interested followers, one of which is written by Mohammad Qutb.

Since 9/11, Sayyid Qutb has become known as "the man who inspired Osama bin Laden." Many of his ideas have apparently surfaced – unacknowledged – in bin Laden's messages, released over the years as he was evading the authorities, although there could have been other texts or interpretations of the Qur'an that explain the link. Writing in the *Guardian*, Karen Armstrong explains, "Bin Laden was not inspired by Wahhabism but by the writings of the Egyptian ideologue Sayyid Qutb, who was executed by President Nasser in 1966. Almost every fundamentalist movement in Sunni Islam has been strongly influenced by Qutb, so there is a good case for calling the violence that some of his followers commit Qutbian terrorism, Qutb urged his followers to withdraw from the moral and spiritual barbarism of modern society and fight it to the death."

One of the ideas shared between bin Laden and Qutb was that Western conflict with Muslims in the Middle East is a continuation of the Crusades – that ostensibly anti-Islamic behavior is not a reaction to events such as terrorism, securing oil interests and so on, but is carried out for ideological reasons: to destroy Islam.

Another was that the U.S. is corrupt, decadent and worthless, a cowardly enemy. In one broadcast, bin Laden states that the U.S. "depends on intense air strikes, which hide its most conspicuous weak points: fear, cowardice and lack of fighting spirit among its troops. These troops are utterly convinced of their government's tyranny and lies, and they know the cause they are defending is not just. They merely fight for capitalists, takers of usury, and arms and oil merchants, including the criminal gang in the White House. Add to that Bush Senior's personal grudges and Crusader hatred."

An extremely religious man before he attended university, bin Laden here encountered the ideology that would fuel his jihad. As well as Sayyid Qutb's reflected glory in the form of his brother, another influential teacher he found was Abdallah Azzam. Azzam had come from Palestine, and would become pivotal in galvanizing Islamic support from around the world for the war against the Soviets in Afghanistan.

If there is one event or period that can be credited with turning Osama bin Laden into a terrorist, it may have occurred in 1979. His time at university had been an eventful one for the Muslim world. Steve Coll writes, "Osama became radicalized in 1979, with the attack of radical Islamists on the Great Mosque in Mecca, the Iranian revolution and the Soviet invasion of Afghanistan. His ego and his ambition grew when, in the Pakistani city of Peshawar, he distributed money, most of it donated by his family, to the Afghan insurgents and then joined the mujaheddin in their holy war."

It may be that the Grand Mosque Seizure was the straw that broke the camel's back: the spark that lit the tinderbox of bin Laden's extremist tendencies and prompted him to final, decisive action. It occurred in November, 1979, when armed insurgents seized control of the Grand Mosque in Mecca: the holiest site in Islam. The dissidents claimed that one of their leaders, a man called Abdullah Hamid Mohammed al-Qahtani, was the Mahdi – the Muslim equivalent of the Messiah, the savior figure who is expected to appear at the end of time.

The terrorist operation was spearheaded by al-Qahtani's brother-in-law, Juhaiman Saif al Otaibi – a wealthy and powerful man who had previously been a corporal in the Saudi National Guard. The two men had been imprisoned together for agitating revolt, and Otaibi is said to have had a vision from God informing him that al-Qahtani was the Mahdi. The purpose of the Grand Mosque Seizure was to force the people to meet their demands of overthrowing the Saudi royal family and creating a theocracy or comprehensive religious law to prepare for the coming end of the world.

The well-planned seizure occurred at the height of the annual *hajj*, or pilgrimage, with the militants taking many pilgrims hostage. Hundreds of people – security forces, insurgents and their hostages – were killed in messy battles as the Saudi state tried to regain the mosque.

The role of the bin Ladens in all this is murky, with sources suggesting that different elements of the extended family took different sides. One of Osama's half brothers was later arrested as a sympathizer, although he was later exonerated. Mahrous bin Laden is said to have helped smuggle weapons into Mecca using trucks belonging to the family business. Imprisoned after the siege ended, he escaped being beheaded – alone among the conspirators – and was eventually released, perhaps only because of the close relationship between the bin Ladens and the royal family. Other sources, however, suggest that the bin Laden family helped the counter-attack by providing blueprints and technical details about the Mosque that were invaluable to its success. The bin Laden company's contract to maintain and renovate the Grand Mosque could easily have enabled them to help either side, and there is such a range of beliefs and approaches among Mohammed's many children that both are certainly possible. Even now, it is said that Mahrous was never given a full say in major business decisions because of his involvement in the plot.

The siege ended two weeks after it began, and only with outside assistance. It was not until the French Special Forces came in – briefly converting to Islam so they could be permitted to set foot in the holy city – that the government was able to regain control. Osama bin Laden was appalled that his government had not been able to take the Mosque back themselves, and had had to rely on non-Muslim foreigners to protect their holiest site. He lost what faith he had left in the Saudi royal family, believing they were weak and corrupt and beyond redemption. When he finished his degree in 1979, he put his money where his mouth was and left for Afghanistan to fight the Soviet invasion.

JIHADI

THE ALLY OF THE CIA

GRADUATING FROM KING Abdulaziz University with a degree in civil engineering in 1979, bin Laden left Jeddah and Saudi Arabia for Afghanistan to join the jihad – the "holy war" – against the Soviet Union. He would use his wealth, ideology and expertise to equip, finance and train the *mujahideen* (freedom fighters; the word comes from the same route as jihad), who were fighting against the Soviet forces deployed to assist Afghanistan's communist government. As well as the native Afghans involved in the conflict, there were many fighters from other Islamic countries. These volunteers were popularly known as Afghan Arabs.

Abdullah Azzam, one of the teachers at his university who had particularly impacted him, had also left Saudi Arabia to head to Peshawar – one of the main border cities of Pakistan and a key location for moving into Afghanistan, to the west. Azzam used this city as a base to organize and equip fighters and arrange their passage through the nearby Khyber Pass into eastern Afghanistan. Initially joining Azzam after he left Jeddah, his old mentor would convince him to use his privilege and money to recruit and train fighters, using a mosque in their vicinity to pull in students and others from the university neighborhood in the area. Bin Laden would spend the next decade there and in Afghanistan, helping the mujahideen in a variety of ways. As well as funding and recruiting, and later engaging the enemy himself, he would use his family's construction equipment to build roads and tunnels through the mountains to assist the Muslim fighters' efforts.

But this wasn't the effort of two men, however well-funded they were thanks to bin Laden's inheritance. In the early 1980s Osama showed his talent for galvanizing wider action and drawing support to his cause. Together they created an organization called Maktab Al-Khadamat – "the Office of Order." The purpose of this was to act as a conduit for money and resources, including weapons, from around the Muslim world to the aspiring mujahideen. Bin Laden's own money and that from supporters would pay for flights and accommodation, and provide the necessary paperwork to satisfy the Pakistani authorities. The BBC recorded, "Egyptians, Lebanese, Turks and others – numbering thousands in bin Laden's estimate – joined their Afghan Muslim brothers in the struggle against an ideology that spurned religion." Bin Laden also established a network of trusted couriers, who carried information between the Afghan front and his base in Peshawar. This network would remain in place for more than twenty years after he left the country.

An enduring source of speculation and controversy is the relationship, if there was one, between bin Laden and the U.S. government in those years. Both the U.S. and bin Laden supported the rebels after the Soviet invasion, with the U.S. providing hundreds of millions of dollars of aid every year to the mujahideen. They were, de facto, on the same side. This fact alone is of no consequence. However, the waters were muddied by the idea that if the U.S. were assisting the mujahideen, they could therefore have collaborated with – perhaps even funded and armed – the man whose Al Qaeda organization would later be responsible for thousands of American deaths.

The U.S. government has always maintained that the CIA only funded native Afghan fighters, and never had any contact with the so-called Afghan Arabs such as bin Laden. CNN's terror analyst, Peter Bergen, claimed that the idea that bin Laden actually worked with the CIA is "simply a folk myth," and that there was no evidence at all to support this theory – a position shared by plenty of other analysts. Nevertheless, other sources have cast doubt on the level of ignorance of, or engagement with, bin Laden's efforts to train and equip the mujahideen. Some of these are based on apparent common sense. The U.S. and bin Laden were, at that point, working towards the same ends – two well-funded, well-organized groups. And, at the time, bin Laden was not known as a terrorist against the West, but as a well-regarded and valuable freedom fighter and a member of Saudi Arabia's most influential family, after the royal family itself. In one 2003 article for the Russian journal *Demokratizatsiya*, Michael Powelson suggested, "It is difficult to believe that the United States played no role in the operations of the son of one of the wealthiest men in Saudi Arabia. Indeed, it is much more likely that the United States knew full-well of bin Laden's operation and gave it all the support they could." Not long after the 9/11 attacks on the Twin Towers, the BBC wrote that the Middle East analyst Hazhir Teimourian stated that bin Laden "received security training from the CIA itself."

Conjecture based on inference, then – that it wasn't possible that two significant groups could operate in the same arena without some overlap – but no hard evidence. Peter Bergen has stressed the differences between their approaches, and the fact that dependence was unnecessary – neither had any need of the other. "In fact, there are very few things that bin Laden, Ayman al-Zawahiri [the new head of Al Qaeda who first met bin Laden in Afghanistan in the 1980s] and the U.S. government agree on. They all agree that they didn't have a relationship in the 1980s. And they wouldn't have needed to. Bin Laden had his own money, he was anti-American and he was operating secretly and independently. The real story here is the CIA did not understand who Osama was until 1996, when they set up a unit to really start tracking him."

It's quite plausible, then, that bin Laden and the CIA didn't cross paths. In fact, as Bergen writes, the truth is arguably more embarrassing. Billions of taxpayer dollars were thrown at the war, but America had no say in how it was spent – it was Pakistani policy that they were not allowed to be involved with the distribution of arms once they were in the country. Bin Laden and the U.S. were coincidentally working toward the same ends at that point – but embarrassingly, he didn't cross their radar until the mid 1990s.

There were other reasons that the CIA would not collaborate with Afghan Arabs. Aside from the fact that there were hundreds of thousands of indigenous Afghans who were more than prepared to fight, the outsiders could be divisive. Milt Bearden, a former CIA official who was active in Afghanistan at that time, summarized that "the Afghans thought they were a pain in the ass." According to cameraman Peter Jouvenal, they could be "more Muslim than thou" and the natives wasted little time on them when they overstepped their limited welcome. "There was no love lost between the Afghans and the Arabs. One Afghan told me, 'Whenever we had a problem with one of them we just shot them. They thought they were kings.'"

In fact, the danger was more than simply one of public relations. At this point, bin Laden had no military experience, and yet his wealth and status meant that he was in charge of similarly untrained Arabs – sometimes with disastrous consequences. Jamal Khalifa spoke of how he fell out with his future brother-in-law over this. "I decided to go myself to see what's going on there. I stayed three days. I started to ask the people how it's going. They said everyday, 'We have plenty of martyrs – people dying.' I said, 'Why?' 'They are not trained and they are very young. They don't have experience and they are facing the Soviets. It's not a joke.'

So I sat down with Osama in his tent underground. I told him, 'Everybody is against this idea. Why are you here? Don't you know that this is very dangerous?' He said, 'We came to be in the front.' I said, 'No, we did not come to be in the front. We came to support Afghans.' I told him, 'Every drop of blood bleeds here in this place. God will ask you about it in the Hereafter. Everybody saying this is wrong, so Osama, please leave the place right now.' Everybody was hearing our argument; our voices become hard. I was really very angry; this is our first time to be like this. I told him, 'Look, you will leave the place or I will never see you again.' He told me, 'Do whatever you want.' So I left."

Bergen concludes, "While the charges that the CIA was responsible for the rise of the Afghan Arabs might make good copy, they don't make good history. The truth is more complicated, tinged with varying shades of gray. The United States wanted to be able to deny that the CIA was funding the Afghan war, so its support was funneled through Pakistan's Inter Services Intelligence agency (ISI). ISI in turn made the decisions about which Afghan factions to arm and train, tending to favor the most Islamist and pro-Pakistan. The Afghan Arabs generally fought alongside those factions, which is how the charge arose that they were creatures of the CIA."

In fact, the Arab Afghans who comprised bin Laden's fighters were "viscerally hostile" to outsiders themselves – especially Westerners who chanced into Afghanistan in the course of reporting the war. In his 2000 book *A Mad World, My Masters*, veteran BBC reporter John Simpson tells of how he met bin Laden in 1989 – before either of them were as well known as they are today. Neither knew who the other was. Simpson recounts how bin Laden offered to pay his Afghan driver five hundred dollars to kill him. It was a significant sum of money for someone in such a poor country, but the man refused. Bin Laden was so frustrated that he returned to his camp bed and wept.

It was almost twenty years before the 9/11 atrocities that bin Laden turned his mind toward the possibility of attacking the U.S. The prompt to his growing unease was the 1982 invasion of Lebanon by Israel. Watching the chaos unfold, bin Laden saw

Beirut's buildings being bombed and destroyed. In a video tape released by Al Jazeera in 2004, he said, "While I was looking at these destroyed towers in Lebanon, it sparked in my mind that the tyrant should be punished with the same and that we should destroy towers in America, so that it tastes what we taste and would be deterred from killing our children and women.

"God knows that it had not occurred to our mind to attack the towers, but after our patience ran out and we saw the injustice and inflexibility of the American-Israeli alliance toward our people in Palestine and Lebanon, this came to my mind." Bin Laden would boycott all American soft drinks, amongst other products, in protest of America's association with Israel, believing that Israel could not have been able to treat the Arab world the way it did without U.S. support. When he had the chance, he put into motion more violent plans.

It was also at this time – during the years that George Bush senior was Vice President (1981-89) and President (1989-93) that he learned to hate the Bush family and what he believed they stood for. He saw the Bush regime as similar to that of repressive Arab governments "in that half of them are ruled by the military and the other half are ruled by the sons of kings and presidents." The elder Bush showed his colors when, during his presidency, he visited Arab countries. "He wound up being impressed by the royal and military regimes and envied them for staying decades in their positions and embezzling the nation's money with no supervision. He passed on tyranny and oppression to his son, and they called it the Patriot Act, under the pretext of fighting terror. Bush the father did well in placing his sons as governors and did not forget to pass on the expertise in fraud from the leaders of the region [i.e. the Middle East] to Florida to use it in critical moments."

BUSINESS AND PLEASURE

JIHAD DID NOT MEAN THE suspension of normal life. In 1983, bin Laden would marry his second wife, a woman called Khadijah Sharif. Nine years older than Osama, she was highly educated and was a university lecturer who worked in Saudi Arabia. She was also said to be a direct descendant of the Prophet Mohammed. The couple would have three children together before separating in the 1990s (paving the way for bin Laden to marry his fifth wife). Bin Laden's head bodyguard, a man called Abu Jandal, would later tell the London based Arab newspaper *Al-Quds Al-Arabi* that the hardships that came with their tough lives were too much for her, and she left to return to Saudi Arabia.

Bin Laden would marry two other women in the 1980s. There was Khairiah Sabar, another highly educated woman and reportedly his favorite wife. She was a child psychologist and had a doctorate in Islamic studies. She was also said to be committed to the jihadi cause and came from a wealthy and well-regarded family. The couple had one son together, Hamza – a leading figure in Al Qaeda and still wanted by the FBI. Khairiah was one of the three wives who were present in the compound in Abbottabad when he was killed. Hamza, although he was apparently living there at the time, managed to escape – the only person missing from the raid. It seems most likely that he was outside the walls at the time of the attack, S-red infrared shots show no figures leaving and no tunnels were found. The fourth woman was Siham

Sabar. She also taught at a university in Saudi Arabia, this time Arabic grammar. She is the mother of Khalid, the son who was killed in Abbottabad, and was also present at bin Laden's death.

Abdallah Azzam was content to co-ordinate support for the mujahideen, using bin Laden's resources and those that came in from around the world through Maktab Al-Khidamat to equip and train fighters. Bin Laden himself became more interested in actually fighting on the front line. Whilst bin Laden wanted the Afghan Arabs to remain a separate unit from the native Afghans, Azzam wanted the two groups to integrate. These differences led to bin Laden part company with the Office of Order around 1988. Instead, he founded a new group that he called Al Qaeda: "The Base."

Al Qaeda is not a homogeneous organization. Its members now spread across the world, with different branches in different geographical regions. Even before bin Laden's death it was fragmented and diverse. It has perhaps been best characterized in the words of the insider Khalid al-Hammadi as "centralization of decision and decentralization of execution."

Its purpose was to bring about the purging of non-Islamic influence in Muslim countries, and the creation of truly Islamic states that conformed to Islamic law. Some of the reported tenets of the group were that Islam was under threat of annihilation from an organized plot led by Jews and Christians – most obviously embodied in the U.S./Israeli alliance – and that killing civilians in the course of jihad is a justified strategy.

Al Qaeda would be a network of independent cells, not a single, top-down organization like Azzam's Office of Order. The cells would act separately, usually without full – or sometimes any – knowledge of each other, making them very difficult to track or stop. Two of its characteristic tactics were suicide bombers, and the simultaneous attacks of different targets. In more recent years, this has been honed in the phenomenon of an initial blast, which causes damage and injury, drawing crowds and emergency services to the location. At this point, a second, larger explosion is set off by a suicide bomber pushing his way into the crowd, causing enormous devastation.

Inasmuch as it can be viewed as a single organization, there were two tiers of membership. Some members took a pledge of loyalty to Osama bin Laden. A list of requirements for membership gleaned from notes made in a meeting between bin Laden and other members in 1988 include "listening ability, good manners, obedience, and making a pledge (*bayat*) to follow one's superiors." But those who took such a pledge were fairly few. More common were those who are considered 'linked' to Al Qaeda – who have trained in one of the terrorist camps in Afghanistan, Pakistan, Sudan or Iraq, but who have not formally pledged to obey the leader. This became more common after 9/11, when the hunt for bin Laden pushed Al Qaeda further underground, decentralizing its leadership and isolating each cells from the others. It became something like a franchise, a brand under which different terrorist groups acted.

Shortly after he founded Al Qaeda, bin Laden's former mentor Azzam was killed. When the Soviet Union withdrew from Afghanistan in 1989 bin Laden returned to Saudi Arabia to take up a post with his family's construction business. At this point he also received a sum of cash – part of a one-time payment made to all of his father's heirs – that is reported to be around eight million dollars.

The Saudi Arabia to which he returned did not inspire him. Whilst he had grown more extreme in his faith, he felt that his home country was becoming less conservative. The following year Iraq invaded Kuwait, ultimately leading to the first Gulf War. As had happened before, when the Grand Mosque had been seized by dissidents ten years earlier, the Saudi royal family allowed foreigners into the country to help – something that disgusted bin Laden and only convinced him further of their weakness and willingness to compromise. Now a seasoned fighter himself, he had offered to help, but had been refused. Spurned and unappreciated, he started to write and publish material criticizing the Saudi regime for their collaboration with U.S. infidels and the threat to the cradle of Islam that this represented.

His anti-government activities led to the Saudis first restricting his movement and ultimately revoking his citizenship. He took his four wives with him and moved with his large family to Khartoum, Sudan in 1992. Over the next two years the U.S. and Saudi Arabia would jointly convince the Sudanese government to expel him too – something that would further enrage him and turn him against both America and all who sympathized with the country.

THE WORLD TURNS

BIN LADEN HAD SLOWLY been laying the foundations for his terrorist activities against the U.S. and the West in general over many years. His childhood had instilled in him a deep respect for Islam and a strong piety. At school he had encountered the Muslim Brotherhood, and this had opened a door for his radicalization in university. His family's money and resources had enabled him to carry out a successful campaign against Soviet forces, and for ten years he had fought for and alongside the mujahideen. He had built up formidable networks of men willing to give their lives for Islam and established an organization to apply his ideals uncompromisingly. Coming home, he felt treated as an outsider, eventually hounded from his home country. And so it was that now, armed with the resources and the experience of a lifetime of wealth and a decade of jihad, he turned his anger against the U.S., which he saw as such a corrupting influence and a threat to the faith that he held in such high regard.

The bomb went off at 12:17 P.M. on February 26, 1993. The rented truck had been packed with fifteen hundred pounds of explosives and parked in the underground car park of the North Tower of the World Trade Center. The plan was that it would ruin the tower's foundations, causing it to topple into the South Tower, destroying them both.

The plot had begun in September the year before when the lead perpetrator, Ramzi Yousef, arrived in the U.S. after spending some time at an Afghan training camp. The camp was later linked to Al Qaeda. He was traveling with another man, Ahmed Ajaj, whose sole purpose was to get caught by immigration inspectors in order to draw attention away from Yousef. When his badly forged passport aroused suspicion and his luggage searched, officials found bomb-making material and other documents. Ajaj is currently serving a one hundred fifteen-year sentence for his part in the plot. When Ajaj was arrested, Yousef walked out of the airport a free man to join his fellow conspirators.

Five months later, Yousef and two other men put together the device. It was a complex bomb, though its core component was a urea nitrate charge – a fertilizer bomb like the IEDs or improvised explosive devices employed by the Taliban to such devastating effect. Around this main charge was packed a mixture of metallic particles – aluminum, magnesium and iron oxide – as well as dynamite as a booster explosive. These materials were packed into cardboard boxes and set with twebty-foot fuses which, Yousef believed, would give him around twelve minutes to escape after lighting them. Finally, three tanks of compressed hydrogen gas were placed around the charges. The result was a thermobaric bomb: a fuel-air device that is significantly more powerful than traditional high explosives. Thermobaric bombs use oxygen from the atmosphere rather than contained in the mix itself. The blast wave they create is longer and more damaging that conventional explosives. Their properties mean they are not suitable for some applications, like underwater demolition. In confined spaces, however – such as the garage of the World Trade Center – they can be devastating.

Yousef lit the fuse and left the building. His hope was that the blast would create a fire that would choke the inhabitants, causing a slow and painful death. He later admitted that he regretted not adding cyanide to the chemical mix. After the blast and fires had done their work, he intended that the tower would collapse, taking its neighbor with it.

The explosion ripped through five of the floors beneath the World Trade Center, causing substantial structural damage – a hundred-foot hole opened across four floors of concrete. The bomb knocked out the power and the lights, plunging the building into darkness. Smoke rushed up the staircases in both towers.

After the second, more destructive bombing of the World Trade Center, the BBC republished the article they had written about the 1993 attack. It shows how this was a taste of things to come – an event that came out of nowhere but would set the tone for the years to come. "The bombing has shocked America which had seemed immune from acts of terrorism that have plagued other parts of the world. An emotional Mario Cuomo, New York's state governor, told journalists: 'We all have that feeling of being violated. No foreign people or force has ever done this to us. Until now we were invulnerable.'" More chilling, there was the comment from one eyewitness, "It felt like an airplane hit the building."

Six people and one unborn baby died that day, and more than one thousand others were injured – many due to smoke inhalation as they tried to escape down the dark staircases. It is possible that Yousef's strategy would have succeeded if he had parked the van closer to the building's foundations, but – for reasons still unknown – he did not. He left America and fled to Pakistan. It took another three years to find and arrest him, and bring him back to the U.S. to face charges. He was found guilty in 1997 and is now serving a two hundred forty-year sentence at a Supermax prison in Florence, Colorado. It is reported that he is eating pork – a meat considered unclean in Islam – and claims to have converted to Christianity.

Yousef's involvement in the first World Trade Center bombing would have been clear without the additional evidence against him. Both before and after he lit the fuses he sent a number of letters to the authorities admitting responsibility and stating his demands and motives, including an end to U.S. involvement with Israel and any interference in the Middle East.

Bin Laden's direct involvement with the plot was and remains unclear. Yousef was the nephew of Khalid Sheikh Mohammed – the lead planner of the 9/11 attacks – and KSM was not, at that point, closely involved with Al Qaeda. He did later admit involvement in the first World Trade Center plot. Although he had met and fought with bin Laden in Afghanistan, it would be some years before they would work together on terror plots. During his prolonged interrogation, KSM said that Yousef was not a member of Al Qaeda and never met bin Laden.

Although the threads of the subsequent inquiry did not explicitly tie bin Laden to the bombing, this seems to have been the point at which he came onto the U.S. administration's radar as a potential threat. There is an enduring narrative that it took until 2001 before the CIA recognized the danger he posed, but this is not true. Even before the 1998 Embassy Bombings in Africa, bin Laden was known as a terrorist. On the second anniversary of 9/11, ten years after the first WTC bombing, investigative journalist Richard Miniter spoke to the *National Review* about his book *Losing bin Laden: How Bill Clinton's Failures Unleashed Global Terror*. "One of the big myths about the Clinton years is that no one knew about bin Laden until Sept. 11, 2001. In fact, the bin Laden threat was recognized at the highest levels of the Clinton administration as early as 1993. What's more, bin Laden's attacks kept escalating throughout the Clinton administration; all told bin Laden was responsible for the deaths of fifty-nine Americans on Clinton's watch. President Clinton learned about bin Laden within months of being sworn into office. National Security Advisor Anthony Lake told me that he first heard the name Osama bin Laden in 1993 in relation to the World Trade Center attack. Lake briefed the president about bin Laden that same year."

Those warnings included information about the contacts and training camps he had developed during his time in Afghanistan, and his plans for using them against the U.S. In fact, it seems that bin Laden might have begun his campaign against America as early as 1992, when he oversaw the bombing of two hotels full of U.S. marines in Yemen.

Miniter states that the way the U.S. authorities dealt with the first WTC bombing hamstrung anti-terrorism attempts. To begin with, at least, it was treated as a criminal investigation – not a terrorist attack. That apparently fine distinction had far-reaching ramifications because it meant that, procedurally; it kept the CIA in the dark about bin Laden. "Once the FBI began a criminal investigation, it could not lawfully share its information with the CIA – without also having to share the same data with the accused terrorists. [Former CIA director] Woolsey told me about his frustration that he had less access to evidence from the World Trade Center bombing – the then-largest ever foreign terrorist attack on U.S. soil – than any junior agent in the FBI's New York office.

"Why did Clinton treat the attack as a law-enforcement matter? Several reasons. In the first few days, Clinton refused to believe that the towers had been bombed at all – even though the FBI made that determination within hours. He speculated an electrical transformer had exploded or a bank heist went bad. More importantly, treating the bombing as a criminal matter was politically advantageous. A criminal matter is a relatively tidy process. It has the political benefit of insulating Clinton from consequences; after all, he was only following the law. He is not to blame if the terrorists were released on a 'technicality' or if foreign nations refuse to honor our extradition requests. Oh well, he tried.

"By contrast, if Clinton treated the bombing as the act of terrorism that it was, he would be assuming personal responsibility for a series of politically risky moves. Should he deploy the CIA or Special Forces to hunt down the perpetrators? What happens if the agents or soldiers die? What if they try to capture the terrorists and fail? One misstep and the media, Congress, and even the public might blame the president. So Clinton took the easy, safe way out, and called it a crime."

Miniter is scathing of Clinton's record on bin Laden, cataloging a long list of failures and opportunities to capture him that were passed over. Not the least of these was his assertion that the 9/11 attacks were planned in May 1998, "on Clinton's watch." Recognizing that this could sound like right-wing propaganda, he argued to the *National Review*, "Most of my best sources were senior Clinton officials, including both of his national-security advisers, his first CIA director, Clinton's counterterrorism czar Richard Clarke, Madeline Albright, and others. Plus, I interviewed scores of career federal officials. None of them are card-carrying members of the vast right-wing conspiracy."

Even if the 1993 bombing could not be laid at bin Laden's feet, there was mounting evidence of terrorists who were linked to him through Al Qaeda, and other jihadi plots that were organized by Al Qaeda – which was now largely made up of the group Egyptian Islamic Jihad. The EIJ was responsible for the attempted assassination of Egyptian Prime Minister Hosni Mubarak in 1995. The association with terror would eventually be too much for bin Laden's family. Already a controversial figure in Saudi Arabia, most of them ultimately severed contact with him – although bin Laden's mother and other members of the family traveled to Afghanistan as late as January 2001 for the wedding of another one of his sons, Mohammed. The family also cut off his annual payment of dividends from the business, said to run to millions of dollars. This in itself was not a major problem. Bin Laden now had access to a network that was more than capable of funding his terrorist activities.

AT HOME AND ABROAD

ALTHOUGH A CLOUD loomed above Osama bin Laden, he was still a free man. In fact, in 1994 he visited London to open what he called the Advice and Reform Committee – in reality the London office of Al Qaeda. This would remain open until 1998, when the U.S. Embassy bombings brought his irrevocable fall from grace. The charges again bin Laden, the director of the London office and nineteen other conspirators read as follows: "In or about 1994, the defendant Osama bin Laden, working together with Khalid al Fawwaz, a/k/a 'Khaled Abdul Rahman Hamad al Fawwaz," a/k/a 'Abu Omar,' a/k/a 'Hamad,' set up a media information office in London, England (hereafter the "London office"), which was designed both to publicize the statements of Osama bin Laden and to provide a cover for activity in support of Al Qaeda's 'military' activities, including the recruitment of military trainees, the disbursement of funds and the procurement of necessary equipment (including satellite telephones) and necessary services. In addition, the London office served as a conduit for messages, including reports on military and security matters from various Al Qaeda cells, including the Kenyan cell, to Al Qaeda's headquarters."

One curious twist to this story is that bin Laden was engaged in more than terrorist recruitment while he was in London. He was said to be an ardent supporter of Arsenal Football Club, and visited their stadium on two occasions. The *Telegraph* newspaper laid out the rumor as follows. "The source is Adam Robinson, in a not otherwise overtly funny or satirical new biography of bin Laden, entitled *Behind the Mask of Terror*, and the story is as follows: that, during the early 1990s, when he was living in London, the man who was later to become the world's most wanted terrorist attended matches at Highbury, in particular during the victorious European Cup-Winners' Cup campaign of the 1993-94 season... It is further alleged that bin Laden visited the Arsenal club shop and bought a replica shirt for one of his sons. Whether, that night in the club shop, bin Laden also bought a Nigel Winterburn duvet cover and some Arsenal shower gel is not recorded. The crucial assertion is this: that Osama is a Gooner." Urban legend or otherwise, there is a serious side to this; bin Laden is said to have used football as a recruitment tool to assess teamwork and spot natural leaders, and to build camaraderie amongst his men.

By now bin Laden had been living in Sudan for two years, setting up home in Khartoum. He was still an outspoken critic of the Saudi regime, and had come to the notice of the Sudanese authorities. By now the Saudis had revoked his citizenship, ensuring that he could not return there. They were also working with the Sudanese to have him expelled from that country, too. When America learned about these efforts, they were enthusiastic supporters. The 9/11 Commission observes that "In late 1995, when bin Laden was still in Sudan, the State Department and the Central Intelligence Agency (CIA) learned that Sudanese officials were discussing with the Saudi government the possibility of expelling bin Laden. CIA paramilitary officer Billy Waugh tracked down bin Laden in the Sudan and prepared an operation to apprehend him, but was denied authorization. U.S. Ambassador Timothy Carney encouraged the Sudanese to pursue this course. The Saudis, however, did not want bin Laden, giving as their reason their revocation of his citizenship. Sudan's minister of defense, Fatih Erwa, has claimed that Sudan offered to hand bin Laden over to the United States. The Commission has found no credible evidence that this was so. Ambassador Carney had instructions only to push the Sudanese to expel bin Laden. Ambassador Carney had no legal basis to ask for more from the Sudanese since, at the time, there was no indictment outstanding." It appears that he may have recognized a more serious threat than the political machinations against him; a failed assassination attempt – perhaps at the hands of either the Saudis or Sudanese regimes – meant that he was no longer safe.

There was also growing U.S. interest and the possible threat of capture by the Americans – although, according to Miniter, this was one of the opportunities that Clinton missed to apprehend the terror chief. "On March 3, 1996, U.S. ambassador to Sudan, Tim Carney, Director of East African Affairs at the State Department, David Shinn, and a member of the CIA's directorate of operations' Africa division met with Sudan's then-Minister of State for Defense Elfatih Erwa in a Rosslyn, Virginia hotel room. Item number two on the CIA's list of demands was to provide information about Osama bin Laden. Five days later, Erwa met with the CIA officer and offered more than information. He offered to arrest and turn over bin Laden himself," Miniter told the *National Review*. "Two years earlier, the Sudan had turned over the infamous terrorist, Carlos the Jackal to the French. He now sits in a French prison. Sudan wanted to repeat that scenario with bin Laden in the starring role."

There are numerous possible reasons why Clinton's officials did not follow through on this offer to hand them bin Laden on a plate. It's possible they thought the offer wasn't serious, or that the Sudanese would or could not actually deliver it. Miniter, though, is harsher in his assessment, arguing that any chance to capture him should have been considered as seriously and actively as possible. "The Clinton administration simply did not want the responsibility of taking Osama bin Laden into custody. Former National Security Advisor Sandy Berger is on the record as saying: 'The FBI did not believe we had enough evidence to indict bin Laden at that time and therefore opposed bringing him to the United States.' Even if that was true – and it wasn't – the U.S. could have turned bin Laden over to Yemen or Libya, both of which had valid warrants for his arrest stemming from terrorist activities in those countries. Given the legal systems of those two countries, Osama would have soon ceased to be a threat to anyone.

"After months of debating how to respond to the Sudanese offer, the Clinton administration simply asked Sudan to deport him. Where to? Ambassador Carney told me what he told the Sudanese: 'Anywhere but Somalia.' "

Bin Laden left Sudan in May 1996 for Afghanistan, quickly establishing a close relationship with Taliban leader Mullah Mohammed Omar. Three months later he openly declared war on the U.S. by issuing the first of two *fatwas*, or pronouncements based on Islamic Law, jointly with a number of other Muslim leaders. Critics within Islam have claimed that bin Laden had no right to do this, since he had not specifically been trained in Islamic Law and was not qualified to offer his opinion. Nevertheless, his point was clear.

The text of the first fatwa was published in the London-based *Al-Quds Al-Arabi* and was called "Declaration of War against the Americans Occupying the Land of the Two Holy Places." An extract reads as follows: "It should not be hidden from you that the people of Islam had suffered from aggression, iniquity and injustice imposed on them by the Zionist-Crusaders alliance and their collaborators; to the extent that the Muslims' blood became the cheapest and their wealth as loot in the hands of the enemies. Their blood was spilled in Palestine and Iraq. The horrifying pictures of the massacre of Qana, in Lebanon are still fresh in our memory. Massacres in Tajakestan, Burma, Cashmere, Assam, Philippine, Fatani, Ogadin, Somalia, Erithria, Chechnia and in Bosnia-Herzegovina took place, massacres that send shivers in the body and shake the conscience. All of this and the world watch and hear, and not only didn't respond to these atrocities, but also with a clear conspiracy between the U.S.A. and its allies and under the cover of the iniquitous United Nations, the dispossessed people were even prevented from obtaining arms to defend themselves... Those youths know that their rewards in fighting you, the U.S.A., is double than their rewards in fighting someone else not from the people of the book. They have no intention except to enter paradise by killing you. An infidel, and enemy of God like you, cannot be in the same hell with his righteous executioner... Terrorizing you, while you are carrying arms on our land, is a legitimate and morally demanded duty. It is a legitimate right well known to all humans and other creatures. Your example and our example is like a snake which entered into a house of a man and got killed by him. The coward is the one who lets you walk, while carrying arms, freely on his land and provides you with peace and security."

A second fatwa along the same lines was issued in February 1998, along with the promise that the U.S. would see the results of this very soon. Bolstered by support from other extremist Islamic groups, including Egyptian Islamic Jihad, Al Qaeda's commitment to kill American civilians and military personnel in the course of their "war against Islam" – most notably in support for Israel – was realized with shocking clarity six months later, with the bombing of the U.S. Embassies in Kenya and Tanzania.

The attacks took place on August 7, 1998. Instead of parking trucks full of explosives and leaving, as Yousef had done at the World Trade Center in 1993, suicide bombers were employed this time. Planning was meticulous, with the two trucks arriving at their targets – the embassies in Nairobi, Kenya and Dar es Salaam, Tanzania, within a few minutes of each other, at around 10:30 in the morning. Packed with many tons of high explosives, they were detonated almost simultaneously.

The Nairobi device killed two hundred twelve people and injured more than four thousand others. The blast was funneled through the streets surrounding the embassy, shattering windows more than half a mile away. The toll was lower in Tanzania, since the embassy was further away from the center of the city with few buildings immediately next to it. Eleven died in Dar es Salaam and other eighty-five injured. Appallingly, although the attacks were against American targets, most of the casualties were locals. Twelve of those who died were American, including two CIA officials.

The embassies were bombed exactly eight years to the day since American troops had first been deployed in Saudi Arabia. Suspicion immediately fell on bin Laden and the Egyptian Islamic Jihad leader Ayman al Zawahiri. Al-Zawahiri is now Al Qaeda's new leader. On June 16, 2011 this was "formalized" in a statement from Al Qaeda on a jihadi website: "Sheikh Dr Ayman al-Zawahiri, may God guide him, assumed responsibility as the group's amir [leader]." Zawahiri is not such a charismatic figure as bin Laden or a good fundraiser, but he is experienced in terrorist operations – some believe he was the "operational brains" behind 9/11, with bin Laden bankrolling and overseeing the attack. A week before assuming command of Al Qaeda, Zawahiri had released a video vowing to continue the fight against America and its allies. "The sheikh has departed, may God have mercy on him, to his God as a martyr and we must continue on his path of jihad to expel the invaders from the land of Muslims and to purify it from injustice… Today, and thanks be to God, America is not facing an individual or a group, but a rebelling nation, which has awoken from its sleep in a jihadist renaissance."

The Embassy Bombings propelled bin Laden up the FBI's Ten Most Wanted and Most Wanted Terrorist lists. Less than two weeks later, Clinton launched retaliatory strikes against strategic targets: a terrorist camp in Afghanistan and a pharmaceutical plant in Sudan, believed to be involved in the manufacture of chemical weapons. Bin Laden escaped the strikes. The factory, which produced around half of Sudan's medication, was destroyed.

Clinton also targeted bin Laden's funding network, blocking any financial dealings between America and Al Qaeda, though this process would take longer than the missile strikes.

This was the turning point: the year in which both the U.S. and bin Laden stepped up their efforts against each other, both single-mindedly and doggedly pursuing the other. For thirteen years, bin Laden would evade capture. In the months and years immediately after the embassy bombings he moved frequently to avoid capture or further strikes. In October 2000, Al Qaeda was involved in another major terrorist attack against the U.S. – this time a suicide bombing of the USS Cole, a destroyer that was stationed at the Yemeni port of Aden. A small motorboat was used to transport a shaped charge consisting of several hundred pounds of explosives up to the side of the destroyer, which was detonated next to the galley. The explosion killed seventeen American sailors and injured thirty-nine others.

Richard Clarke, counter-terrorism adviser in the Clinton administration, examined the evidence around the bombing of the Cole and soon came to the conclusion that bin Laden had been behind it. The U.S. responded by offering a five million dollars reward for information leading to his capture. A lawsuit was later filed against the Sudanese government on the grounds that Al Qaeda could not have successfully carried out the attack without assistance from Sudanese officials. But still, bin Laden avoided arrest. Al Qaeda had arguably become the first terrorist organization that was fully independent of any foreign country, thanks to its huge resources. Nevertheless, the Pentagon had developed plans to carry out strikes against Al Qaeda's bases and training camps in Afghanistan. Clarke was all for implementing these, but was voted down by other top officials for various reasons. It was a gray area in international law and some wanted more proof of bin Laden's involvement. There was the potential PR disaster of the world's reaction to a "war against Muslims," and it was felt that such retaliation could set back the Middle

East peace process. Ambassador-at-Large for Counter-terrorism at that time, Michael Sheehan, apparently told Clarke, "What's it going to take to get them to hit Al Qaeda in Afghanistan? Does Al Qaeda have to attack the Pentagon?" The answer was, of course – although they didn't know it at the time – yes.

So, says Miniter, Clinton balked at the last chance to take down bin Laden before 9/11. Politically it was too risky, and with only a few more weeks in office Clinton didn't want to rock the boat. "Instead of destroying bin Laden's terrorist infrastructure and capabilities, President Clinton twice phoned the president of Yemen demanding better cooperation between the FBI and the Yemeni security services. If Clarke's plan had been implemented, Al Qaeda's infrastructure would have been demolished and bin Laden might well have been killed. Sept. 11, 2001 might have been just another sunny day."

At this point, bin Laden was in the thick of his terrorist activities, at the most prolific point in his long campaign against America. Nevertheless, he still found time for a personal life. He had already married four times, though one of those wives had left him some time before when she found their unpredictable, nomadic existence too much to bear. In 2000, he married for a fifth time.

The girl's name – she was little more than a girl at the time – was Amal Ahmed al-Sadah, and she was Osama's youngest wife. Sources suggest she was born in 1981, making her nineteen at the time, although a Yemeni passport has her date of birth as 1987. This is the wife who was later wounded when the SEALs stormed the compound in Abbottabad. At first, it was reported that he had used her as a "human shield"; later, it transpired that one of them had shot her in the leg after she rushed them as they entered the room.

Amal had been born in Yemen, and her marriage to bin Laden was apparently part of his recruitment drive in that country. In

The Looming Tower, Wright suggests that "the marriage seems to have been a political arrangement between bin Laden and an important Yemeni tribe, meant to boost Al Qaeda recruitment in Yemen." She was apparently a gift to bin Laden from her family. Sheikh Rashad Mohammed Saeed Ismael, a bin Laden 'aide' who helped to arrange the marriage, spoke to the UK's *Sunday Times* about the teenage girl. "Even at her young age she was religious and spiritual enough and believed in the things that bin Laden – a very religious, pious and spiritual man – believed in," he said. "Coming from a modest Yemeni family, she could live with him the tough life in mountain caves and be someone he could mold. She was also someone who did not mind marrying a man as old as her father, and truly believed that being a dutiful and obedient wife to her husband would grant her a place in heaven."

Ismael, who lived in the same town in Yemen as the woman and her father, a civil servant, said that he met with her to obtain her consent to the match. "I told her: You know of bin Laden, who gave away his palaces and fortune to wage jihad on behalf of Muslims. He lives in Afghanistan, sometimes in fear for his life, sometimes secured; sometimes in a city and a house, at other times in a mountain and a cave on the run." Her father gave permission for bin Laden to take her away to Afghanistan to marry him. In return, bin Laden is said to have paid around five thousand dollars in clothes and jewelry to the family. *Time* reports that although he was already at the top of the Most Wanted list even then, they considered it a great honor that she was marrying him.

However, it is worth noting that all of this occurred before 9/11. At this stage, bin Laden did not have the notoriety he did afterwards. His fight against the Soviet invaders of Afghanistan through the 1980s informed his reputation far more than any terrorist activities. "In 1999, bin Laden was respected as a freedom fighter and fought against the Soviet occupation," Amal's brother told the *Telegraph* after bin Laden's death. "This was before September 11. That is why my father consented to the match. He was not a wanted man then. No one considered him to be a terrorist." The family naturally has an interest in rewriting history, but has stated that Amal's faith was devout but not extremist. "She has always been a very kind and polite girl. She was absolutely my parents' favorite daughter, and I remember how she used to gather us and give us lectures on good Islamic manners and taught us how to be kind to others. Once when we were children, we went to throw stones at our neighbors from the roof. Amal found out about it and told us off, reminding us how the Prophet ordered us to treat others with kindness." After the raids, the Sada family expressed their concern that Amal might remain in prison indefinitely due to her connection with bin Laden and possible information she might have about Al Qaeda. "My mother cries constantly," said Sada. "At first, it was reported that she had actually been killed, and that put our family through undue suffering. However, we know that if the U.S. wanted to get rid of Amal, they would have simply killed her along with bin Laden. That fact eases our worries slightly. But Amal had nothing to do with Al Qaeda or terrorism of any kind. No law can incriminate her, and international law dictates that she should be returned to her family."

If she does ever return home to Yemen, it will be the first time she has seen her family for more than a decade. After the marriage, Amal may have moved around with bin Laden or she may have been more settled. Two years after the marriage, she spoke a little about her life as one of four wives to *Al-Majallah*, a London-based Arabic news service. "Each wife lived in her own house. There were two wives in Kandahar, each with her own house," MSNBC quoted her. "The third wife had a house in Kabul, and the fourth in the Tora Bora mountains. He used to come to me once a week. His wives met only once every month or two when he came to us or sent one of his sons to take us to one of the others' houses."

Bin Laden was a lonely figure, by her account. She said that he would come home late "and lie down alone on his bed for long hours... He did not like anybody to talk to him. He became angry if I tried to talk to him and I would therefore leave him alone. He used to sit and think for a long time and sleep very late. He did not sleep for more than two or three hours at a time. Though he was beside me, I sometimes felt lonely."

She was one of three wives – the other two being Siham Sabar and Khairiah Sabar – who moved into the compound in Abbottabad, where it is thought he lived for at least five years. That mixture of wives, old and young, is said to have caused predictable tensions. "She was new. She was out of place. The Sheikh's other wives were much older than she was. So were many of his sons," the *Mail* quoted one source.

Amal and the other women were taken into the custody of the Pakistani intelligence service, the ISI. One former ISI commander, Asad Munir, told *ABC News* that they would be involved in "non-violent interviews." "We give them a questionnaire, with twenty questions. We change the order of questions every three or four days. For telling lies you have to have very good memory. There's a way to find out. No one will tell you the first day the correct answer."

Other reports suggest that the three widows "are turning on each other in custody, with two older Saudi women blaming a much younger Yemeni wife for leading American intelligence to their hideout," as the *Australian* puts it. "It's vicious," said a Pakistani official briefed on the interrogation of the widows. "The older wives think the younger one tipped off the Americans or was tracked when she came to join him." Pakistani officials who have been debriefing the women portray life in the compound as an Islamic version of Desperate Housewives. "It's a well-known fact that when you have two older wives and then this young one comes along half their age, they don't like it," said one. The wives even dispute who tried to protect their husband in the raid. The youngest was reported to have attempted to save him, sustaining a bullet wound to her calf. But the older wives say they were the ones who rushed to shield him." Rehman Malik, Pakistan's Interior Minister has suggested another alternative. "The joke in Pakistan is that bin Laden called in his location to CIA because he was being driven mad cooped up for five years with so many wives and children."

The infuriating thing is that none of this – the raid on the compound, the years of searching, even 9/11 itself – need to have happened. There were a number of opportunities to kill or capture bin Laden before 9/11 – in the period when he shot into the awareness of the U.S. authorities after the Embassy Bombings in Kenya and Tanzania, and with the suicide attack on the USS Cole, but before that final, catastrophic attack on U.S. soil that triggered two wars in the Middle East and countless further civilian and military deaths. Bin Laden biographer Steve Coll comments, "It would have been possible to eliminate Osama bin Laden, specifically between 1998 and 2001, in the time before Sept. 11. We had agents on site at the time, and they gave Clinton the chance to strike three times. One time he decided against a missile attack, because he was unwilling to accept the deaths of children. A swing was distinguishable on a satellite image of bin Laden's base near Kandahar. It probably would also have been possible to surround the camp with Special Forces and extract him. But those weren't the political priorities at the time. But even after 9/11 there was an opportunity. Bin Laden himself later wrote about how desperate his situation was during the heavy bombing of his cave hideout in Tora Bora near the Pakistani border in December 2001. He managed to escape at the last minute. Whether some of the Afghan troops that had advanced with U.S. troops into the mountains were simply too half-hearted or actively helped him get away, it's hard to say. In any event, we neglected to bring in the Tenth Mountain Division, which specialized in that type of combat and was partly stationed in Uzbekistan at the time. It was a bad decision."

And it was that series of bad decisions and underestimation of bin Laden's evil and influence that led to what was probably the defining event of a generation, the suicide attacks on American soil that led to the destruction of the World Trade Center and thousands of deaths.

THE TWIN TOWERS

AL QAEDA'S MASTER PLAN

SEPTEMBER 11, 2001 was the day the world changed. Now ten years past, the events of that day still reverberate across the United States and across the world in almost every aspect of foreign policy and much of domestic.

9/11 woke the West up to the unfathomable threat of extremist terrorism, alerted them to the fragility of their safety, and forever colored their view of Islam. No other single event in a generation and possibly a century has so shaken the foundations of society than the suicide attacks on the Twin Towers of the World Trade Center, the Pentagon and the Capitol Building, organized by the Saudi-born jihadi who was already the FBI's Most Wanted Man, Osama bin Laden.

The targets were all large buildings, iconic to America and emblazoned in the national consciousness. They stood for prosperity, democracy and justice. As such, they were highly symbolic as well as strategic in terms of casualty numbers. The White House was apparently a target that had been considered for the same reasons, but it was rejected on the grounds that it would be difficult to see from the air. Al Qaeda figures who were captured after 9/11 have stated that there may have been a further plan in progress that would use a GPS to locate the White House from a plane. Richard Reid, the "shoe bomber" later arrested for trying to detonate a bomb on American Airlines Flight 63 in December 2001, was named in conjunction with this plot, though prosecutors are doubtful about the veracity of the evidence. The later shoe-bomb plan only failed because flight delays meant the fuses in his boot had absorbed sweat and rainwater, and were too damp to ignite; Reid is now serving life without parole in a supermax prison.

9/11 was Osama bin Laden's biggest triumph, and one of America's darkest hours. The plot had been in development for five years. It was, as a concept, not bin Laden's own idea. The initial plan for crashing hijacked airplanes into high-value targets had originated with Khalid Sheikh Mohammed, one of Al Qaeda's most senior operatives.

Khalid Sheikh Mohammed – often known simply as KSM – had come to the U.S. authorities' attention in 1995 in a plot to destroy U.S. planes over the Pacific Ocean. The plan was known as Operation Bojinka, and had also involved KSM's nephew, Ramzi Yousef, who had been responsible for the 1993 World Trade Center bombing. Bojinka was funded by Al Qaeda. It had only failed because police found computer files linked to the operation when they were investigating a separate but related plot to assassinate the Pope.

Bojinka was a tremendously complex and ambitious plot – probably the reason it failed. It was multi-phased, intended to cause enormous chaos through a crescendo of terror. The idea was that this would begin with the assassination of Pope John Paul II. It would also involve the bombing of eleven or twelve airplanes over the Pacific. Subsequent stages of the plan would involve crashing small airplanes – laden with explosives – into strategic targets such as the CIA headquarters. The discovery of documents detailing the plan led to the arrest of Ramzi Yousef, but his uncle KSM escaped and remained at large for another ten years. During this time he developed and refined Bojinka into what would become the devastating attacks of 9/11.

KSM ended up in Afghanistan after a brief stay in Qatar that had to be cut short when the U.S. demanded his arrest and extradition. This was 1996, the time when bin Laden himself was seeking a safe haven from the interest of the authorities and leaving Sudan in order to carry out his war against America and its allies.

KSM and bin Laden had met before – indeed, they had fought together against the Soviets in Afghanistan toward the end of the 1980s. However, they were not especially close and had not seen each other since bin Laden left the country to return to Saudi Arabia in 1989. KSM used one of his contacts to arrange a meeting between them, knowing that their interests overlapped significantly and that they might be able to work together in their shared battle. He has suggested that the fame of his nephew, Ramzi Yousef, played a part in convincing the Al Qaeda leader to meet with him. The meeting was arranged to take place in Tora Bora, the inaccessible mountainous region on the Afghan/Pakistan border that bin Laden knew well from the days of the Soviet War.

Khalid Sheikh Mohammed was an ideas man. Others had the resources to pull off his schemes, but he was the one with the plan – a highly versatile and experienced terrorist. The 9/11 Commission writes, "No one exemplifies the model of the terrorist entrepreneur more clearly than Khalid Sheikh Mohammed, the principal architect of the 9/11 attacks. KSM followed a rather tortuous path to his eventual membership in Al Qaeda. Highly educated and equally comfortable in a government office or a terrorist safe house, KSM applied his imagination, technical aptitude, and managerial skills to hatching and planning an extraordinary array of terrorist schemes. These ideas included conventional car bombing, political assassination, aircraft bombing, hijacking, reservoir poisoning, and, ultimately, the use of aircraft as missiles guided by suicide operatives."

He presented bin Laden and other Al Qaeda leaders (including the Egyptian Mohammed Atef, Al Qaeda's military leader, who had been closely involved with the Embassy Bombings) with a range of ideas – including refined versions of Operation Bojinka, which had involved flying small planes loaded with explosives into high-value targets. This time, he suggested, it might be better to hijack commercial airliners and fly them into buildings. KSM also told bin Laden and the other leaders about the plots he had helped mastermind, including the first World Trade Center bombing. The two ideas were juxtaposed, and the beginnings of the 9/11 plot were formed.

KSM knew that he didn't stand a chance of carrying off such an attack without the resources that Al Qaeda had to offer. Aside from the question of the significant funding that such a project would require, he needed men and he needed logistical support. He knew that bin Laden shared his hatred of America, and believed that he had found a willing co-conspirator.

He would have to wait. Reports suggest that bin Laden listened to the ideas, but didn't say much – although other members of Al Qaeda were enthusiastic. At this point, he was still shaping his anti-America strategy, and wasn't ready to decide on a particular plan. He did ask KSM to bring his family to Afghanistan and invited him to join Al Qaeda, but KSM preferred to keep his options open. There were other jihadi groups operating in Afghanistan, and joining Al Qaeda might prejudice his chances of joining these too. The situation in the country was complex, with different rival groups. Bin Laden was forging ties with the Taliban, whereas KSM hoped to work with others who would not necessarily view that link as positive. For now, the two would go their separate ways, with KSM ending up in Pakistan, amongst other places.

It was two years later that bin Laden oversaw the bombing of the two U.S. embassies in Kenya and Tanzania. Under his prolonged interrogation, Khalid Sheikh Mohammed would later admit that this was the point at which he realized that bin Laden was committed to his war against America. Al Qaeda was a major player, it turned out, and he could achieve more with this one group than with any of the others with which he had associated in preference to bin Laden's organization. So it was that he ingratiated himself with Al Qaeda, in ways such as helping them to update their old computers. He would officially join Al Qaeda in 1998, although he says that he never swore the personal oath of allegiance to Osama bin Laden.

All the while, he was developing the idea he had first attempted to pioneer with Operation Bojinka – as well as further plots in Israel and other countries. The original plan he had pitched to bin Laden was complex and quite clearly too ambitious. It had involved hijacking ten airplanes and crashing them into five targets on the West Coast and five on the East Coast. The commercial airliners, he realized, were easier to manage than smaller planes packed with explosives. His work with Yousef planning the first attack on the World Trade Center had showed him that bombs were not always practical. They could be unpredictable and, of course, risked discovery – especially if there was a period between positioning and detonating them. The World Trade Center plan had ultimately failed because Yousef had parked the truck in the wrong place. Although the damage had been extensive, the towers remained standing. There was the possibility that Yousef also delayed his mission for a few hours because of security problems. These were all variables that could not be controlled. KSM knew that a simpler plan would be more reliable. Airplanes – especially large ones – would be practically unstoppable once they were in the air. And, he realized, there was no need to pack them with explosives, which was the original plan. The full tank of jet fuel would be just as effective once they collided with their targets. The tremendous kinetic energy of a large plane in flight – moving at several hundred miles per hour and weighing many tons – would be destructive enough in its own right. Add to that the explosion of thousands of gallons of fuel and there was a recipe that was far more effective than a small plane loaded with a bomb.

KSM brought up his idea with the Al Qaeda leadership as he rose within the hierarchy. Mohammed Atef, the organizations military leader, eventually brought the idea up with bin Laden himself and convinced the terror chief to reconsider. Bin Laden gave what would become the 9/11 plot his attention, consideration and ultimately full backing late in 1998 or early 1999 – including providing some of the necessary personnel. However, he too recognized that simple was better, and vetoed the ten-plane plan. Instead, they eventually agreed on hijacking four airliners, picking four high-value targets.

It was at this point that the plot first came to the notice of the U.S. government; in December 1998, counter-terrorism officials told the then President Clinton that Al Qaeda was planning to attack the U.S., and that a plot might involve hijacking airplanes. KSM and bin Laden met a number of times early in 1999 to hone the plan. KSM's role has been described as "operational support": organizing travel and other arrangements for the hijackers, helping to choose targets, and so on. It seems that KSM's plans were grandiose and perhaps too expensive and time-consuming; bin Laden's role on a number of occasions appears to have been reining him in, cutting the ideas down to a manageable size and, in the process, ensuring that they were realistic enough to work. One of the early targets KSM put forward was the U.S. Bank Tower in Los Angeles, with bin Laden vetoed.

Bin Laden helped plan the mission and he bankrolled it through Al Qaeda, but it was not until two years after 9/11 that the U.S. authorities realized the full scale of his role. He was more active and more directly involved than had previously been believed. The *New York Times* summarized: "A classified government analysis circulated this week among counterterrorism officials said Khalid Sheikh Mohammed, the captured Qaeda leader, has told interrogators that Mr. bin Laden gave Mohammed Atta, the leader of the Sept. 11 hijackers, 'a list of targets.' The document said it included the World Trade Center, the Pentagon, the United States Capitol, the White House, the Israeli Embassy in Washington and the Sears Tower in Chicago. Officials are trying to determine if the statements by Mr. Mohammed are true. In some interrogations, officials said, Qaeda detainees have purposely spread disinformation."

Along with the finance and oversight, bin Laden hand-picked some of the men to hijack and fly the planes. Two of those he chose were Nawaf al-Hazmi and Khalid al-Mihdhar – jihadis who had fought in Bosnia and who he believed he could rely on. They would attend flying lessons in California after arriving in the U.S. early in 2000, but showed little aptitude. Their English was also bad, and they were demoted to the secondary status of 'muscle' hijacker. A more promising man was Hani Hanjour, who already had a commercial pilot's license before becoming involved with Al Qaeda. New recruits to Al Qaeda were vetted for their suitability, and any special skills – as in the case of Hanjour – were noted. Four other men were picked thanks to their experience of living in Europe or America and their better command of English.

The so-called "planes operation," as it was known in Al Qaeda, was significantly larger than the version deployed late in 2001. As late as the spring of 2000, there was another strand to the plan that involved crashing planes into Asian targets on the same day. In addition, KSM still planned to use six planes, rather than four. Bin Laden shelved these ideas when they could not find the men to fly them, and when the difficulties of planning the attacks on both continents became too great.

The Day the World Changed

THE EVENTS OF SEPTEMBER 11, 2001 are known in staggering detail thanks to the diligent work of the security services and the coming-of-age of the Internet, which meant that information could be accessed and shared almost instantly across the world.

The whole operation was tightly planned and well executed. At 7:59 A.M., American Airlines Flight 11 – a fully fueled Boeing 767 – took off from Logan International Airport, carrying five hijackers. It left fourteen minutes later than scheduled on its flight from Boston to Los Angeles. Once in the air, the terrorists wasted little time. It was just fifteen minutes later that air traffic controllers ordered the plane to climb to thirty-five thousand feet, but received no reply.

At the same moment, at 8:14, a similar plane – United Airlines Flight 175 – left the tarmac of Boston Logan Airport, also heading for Los Angeles, also carrying five hijackers. With two planes now in the air, it was five long minutes before information filtered through about the first flight. One of the flight attendants on Flight 11, a woman called Betty Ong, managed to alert the airline using a phone. "The cockpit is not answering, somebody's stabbed in business class – and I think there's Mace – we can't breathe. I don't know, I think we're getting hijacked."

Just one minute later, as flight controllers realized they were dealing with a hijack situation, the third plane – American Airlines

Flight 77 – left the ground at Washington Dulles International Airport, also bound for LA. Again, five hijackers were on board.

In the first plane, the hijackers were familiarizing themselves with the cockpit and taking strategic decisions about how best to delay any response. They turned the transponder off, although the plane was still visible to radar. A few minutes later, at 8:24, they accidentally made a radio transmission when the new pilot, Mohammed Atta, held the wrong button down. Instead of talking to the passengers, the message was broadcast to air traffic controllers: "We have some planes. Just stay quiet, and you'll be okay. We are returning to the airport... nobody move. Everything will be OK. If you try to make any moves, you'll endanger yourself and the airplane. Just stay quiet." Two minutes after this chilling message, Atta guided the plane into a 100-degree turn to the south, pointing it towards its final destination, New York City.

The last plane – the now-famous United Airlines Flight 93 – had been delayed longer than the others, but at 8:42 it took off from Newark International Airport for San Francisco, forty minutes late. This time, only four hijackers were on board, which would later raise the question that perhaps there was originally supposed to be another man in the 9/11 plot, the "20th hijacker."

Had the plane departed on time, it would have been in the air before any problems were recognized with Flight 11. As it was, the four hijackers must have spent the extra time sweating that their flight would be grounded and their part in the plot foiled. It was not to be, but those forty minutes may have had a very significant effect: they allowed time of the news about the first planes to filter through to the passengers, who fought back. Realistically, once the planes were in the air there was very little chance of them landing safely. But those forty minutes may have saved the Capitol Building and many more lives on the ground.

The full magnitude of the plot was still not understood at this point, barely forty-five minutes after the first plane had taken off. A few minutes earlier, the second plane to fly – United Airlines

Flight 175 – had notified controllers that the pilots had sighted the hijacked Flight 11, some ten miles to their south. Moments after the last plane left the tarmac, 175 was hijacked.

On board Flight 11, the crew and passengers had realized that something was badly wrong. This was not an ordinary hijacking. One of the flight attendants, Amy Sweeney, managed to get a call through to American Airlines. "Something is wrong. We are in a rapid descent... we are all over the place." The man she was speaking to asked her what she could see out of the window. "I see the water. I see the buildings. I see buildings... We are flying low. We are flying very, very low. We are flying way too low." There was a long pause, and then – her final words – "Oh my God, we are way too low."

Her call was cut off at 8:46 when the plane collided with the North Tower of the World Trade Center. It hit the north side a little above the 90th floor, traveling at around 466 miles per hour. The effect of a fully-fueled Boeing 767 smashing into the skyscraper was devastating. It remained intact, its tremendous momentum carrying it right to the center of the building – the structural core of the tower – and sending an immense shock-wave up and down the superstructure. Fuel from the ruptured tanks flooded out and ignited, setting light to the plane, debris and everything around them. Worse, the already damaged concrete core was super-heated, progressively weakening it and decreasing its ability to hold the weight above it as every minute passed. Everyone below the impact area began to run for the staircases. No one above could make their way down, since the plane had severed all three stairwells.

No one saw this impact on live TV; there were no professional camera crews present to report what was going on, because at this stage, no one knew anything. As the news worked its way through to the stations, they realized that something big was happening and scrambled their crews.

Fox's WNYW was the first station on the scene with cameras, and lost no time broadcasting the towering monolith, smoke and flames pouring out of the impact site. At this stage, no one had much idea about what was going on. WNYW hurried to get the news out, with the reporter giving off-the-cuff commentary based only on what he could see and infer (not always accurately; to begin with, he mistook which tower had been hit). "Just a few moments ago, something believed to be a plane crashed into the South Tower of the World Trade Center. I just saw flames inside, you can see the smoke coming out of the tower; we have no idea what it was. It was a tremendous boom just a few moments ago. You can hear around me emergency vehicles heading towards the scene. Now this could have been an aircraft or it could have been something internal. It appears to be something coming from the outside, due to the nature of the opening on about the 100th floor of the South Tower of the World Trade Center."

If it was chaos on the ground, the situation in the tower itself was worse. Everyone who could evacuate did so. Those above the impact zone did not have the option. Some rushed upwards, hoping to be rescued from the roof, but no rescue attempt ever materialized or was even possible. The smoke pouring from the shattered tower was too thick to risk landing a helicopter on the roof, which was in any case too hot to put down on. Horizontal rescue from the side of the tower was impossible with the helicopters and equipment available.

One of the most appalling sights of 9/11 was the series of men and women who chose to jump from the stricken building, knowing that the quick death from the fall would be preferable to burning to death or slowly choking on the smoke in the tower. Somewhere between one hundred and two hundred fifty people across the two towers eventually chose to end their lives this way, taking the only form of control they could in a situation with few options available to them. A further death occurred on the ground when a firefighter was struck by one of those who jumped from one hundred floors up.

Even at this point, no one realized the full extent of the attacks, terrible though it had already been. A couple of minutes later, the third flight – Flight 77 – was hijacked. At the same time, a passenger on Flight 175 made a cellphone call to his father, telling him that someone had been killed, the cockpit had been taken, and the plane was now moving erratically. In the still-intact South Tower of the World Trade Center, panic reigned. An announcement was made over the PA system instructing its occupants to return to their offices because the building was secure, but many ignored it. Although some evacuated, others gathered in communal areas to try to find out more. Meanwhile, the hijackers on Flight 175 had changed its heading for New York, destined for the second tower.

Fragmentary information was now being pieced together from multiple sources – cellphone calls from the planes, information about the collision, and transponder and radar data. At least one of the remaining aircraft had essentially disappeared from sight to the aviation authorities after the hijackers turned off or altered the frequencies of the transponders, and air traffic control was searching open space.

By the time the authorities realized that they had a complex attack on their hands, it was too late. Just after 9 A.M. a manager at the Federal Aviation Administration in New York warned the Air Traffic Control System Command Center, "We have several situations going on here. It's escalating big, big time. We need to get the military involved with us... We're involved with something else, we have other aircraft that may have a similar situation going on here." One minute later, at 9:03, Flight 175 hit its target: the south face of the South Tower of the World Trade Center. This time, it was lower down and banking sharply when it struck – the pilot trying to ensure a square impact rather than a glancing blow – meaning that the wings spanned more floors.

The impact zone spread from floors seventy-seven to eighty-five and fragments of the plane – which was traveling at five hundred ninety miles per hour – broke away and fell up to six blocks away.

With many news cameras now recording the effects of the first strike at the North Tower, the second impact was caught on live television and instantly broadcast to millions of dumbstruck viewers. And yet still they did not immediately realize what they were witnessing. Those from the right vantage point saw the second plane fly in; others, with the North Tower obscuring the view of the South, believed a second explosion had taken place at the original crash site. The misinformation they broadcast was swiftly corrected by eyewitness accounts, and the full enormity of what was happening became clear. Even then, some broadcasters suggested that it was a freak accident caused by the failure of the planes' navigation systems. Others had realized that there was no other explanation than a terrorist attack.

In Florida, President George W. Bush was embarking on a tour of an elementary school. His aides informed him of the first collision, but he decided to continue with his planned itinerary. Much has been made of his reaction, and his reaction to news of the second collision. He was opening a book to read to the second-grade students – a story called *The Pet Goat* – when his Chief of Staff, Andrew Card, whispered to him: "A second plane hit the second tower. America is under attack." Bush remained where he sat, reading with the students, for several minutes longer before he gave a short press conference at the school during which he spoke about the attacks. He was then taken to a secure location, since no one knew what was going on or whether there would be further attacks.

Bush was harshly criticized for staying where he was, despite knowing that his country was under attack. He later justified his actions by stating that he wanted everyone to stay calm, and that abruptly leaving the second-graders would have sent a message that something was wrong and that people were panicking. The comedian and social commentator Michael Moore was particularly critical, using the episode to demonstrate Bush's ineptness and unsuitability for the presidency. He was joined by many others – including, three years later, Osama bin Laden himself. In 2004, bin Laden released a video message in which he poured scorn on Bush for such an error of judgment. "It never occurred to us that the commander in chief of the American armed forces would leave fifty thousand of his citizens in the two towers to face these horrors alone. It appeared to him that a little girl's talk about her goat and its butting was more important than the planes and their butting of the skyscrapers. That gave us three times the required time to carry out the operations, thank God," he said.

The *Washington Post* detailed the frantic discussions that were occurring between high-level officials as they tried to limit the damage. "Transportation Secretary Norman Y. Mineta, summoned by the White House to the bunker, was on an open line to the Federal Aviation Administration operations center, monitoring Flight 77 as it hurtled toward Washington, with radar tracks coming every seven seconds... Mineta shouted into the phone to Monte Belger at the FAA: "Monte, bring all the planes down." It was an unprecedented order – there were 4,546 airplanes in the air at the time. Belger, the FAA's acting deputy administrator, amended Mineta's directive to take into account the authority vested in airline pilots. "We're bringing them down per pilot discretion," Belger told the secretary. "**** pilot discretion," Mineta yelled back. "Get those goddamn planes down.""

New York airspace was finally closed to all commercial flights, and shortly afterward all NYC-area airports were closed, but by now it was too late: the damage had been done. As with the first tower, those people above the impact line in the North Tower had no means of escape – or, at least, few of which they were aware. In fact, one stairwell remained intact, but misinformation meant that only a handful of people found it. Many ran to the roof hoping for an aerial rescue that was all but impossible under the conditions. Not long later, flights were grounded nationally. Again, it was too late: all of the relevant airplanes were in flight.

As Bush was giving his press conference in the elementary school, hijackers were taking over Flight 93 and securing the cockpit. The president simply stated that the U.S. was experiencing a national tragedy, and that he was returning to Washington to oversee the disaster. There was little more to say; he had no more information than anyone else. After a moment of silence, shared by the audience of two hundred students and teachers, he left.

On the remaining two flights, the hijackers were using a range of tactics to keep order. In the absence of information to the contrary, the passengers believed that this was just a regular hijacking, not a suicide mission. The terrorists told them that they had a bomb on board, a message intended to ensure co-operation.

Aviation authorities realized that there might be further collisions, a possibility that took on a terrible new likelihood when they lost contact with Flight 77. They notified the Secret Service at the White House that another aircraft was heading their direction and they could not talk to the cockpit. Just as Secret Service were preparing to evacuate the building, the aircraft changed course, heading towards Reagan International Airport.

The reprieve was short-lived. Only a minute later, the plane changed course again. Secret Service took the Vice President, Dick Cheney, down to a security bunker, but the hijackers weren't interested in the White House. Instead, they crashed the plane into the west side of the Pentagon, a little over two miles away. This target was more symbolic; the different structure of the Pentagon meant that it would not collapse like the towers, and the comparatively low height meant that evacuation was easier. As it happened, the plane also crashed into a part of the building that had recently been refurbished, and the offices were mainly empty. Still, one hundred twenty-five people died on the ground, as well as all sixty-four on the plane.

Secretary of Defense Donald Rumsfeld himself was in the building at the time. "In his Pentagon office, Rumsfeld felt the huge building shudder," records the *Washington Post*. "He looked out his window, then rushed out toward the smoke, running down the steps and outside where he could see pieces of metal strewn on the ground. Rumsfeld began helping with the rescue efforts until a security agent urged him to get out of the area. 'I'm going inside,' he said, and took up his post in the National Military Command Center, the Pentagon war room."

Less than an hour after the first impact, at 9:59 A.M., the South Tower began its collapse. Had the towers been built along more traditional lines, they might have remained standing. However, the two tallest towers of the World Trade Center complex had been designed in such a way as to maximize open, useful space for the workers. The skyscrapers were "framed tube structures." That is, they were built around a core of supports in the center, stretching up the height of the building, with a second ring of supports around the perimeter – like a tube within a tube. That meant that there didn't need to be any other pillars elsewhere in the usable space, breaking it up and making it less flexible for the occupants. The weight of the floors – four inch thick concrete slabs supported on a steel frame – was shared between the core tube and one around the outer edges of the building. At the time (the towers were designed in the 1960s and completed in the early 1970s) they were ground-breaking, and the dual 110-floor towers were the tallest in Manhattan.

Interestingly, a number of engineers had considered what might happen if a plane collided with the World Trade Center, including its lead structural engineer. After all, it wasn't inconceivable – in 1945 a B-25 bomber had crashed into the Empire State Building after the pilot became disoriented in fog. The engineers concluded that the greatest risk would be the fire that resulted from ruptured fuel tanks flooding the building with burning fuel, but that the structure itself would survive. Perhaps they were wrong, but no one had considered the possibility of a fully-fueled 767 being deliberately flown into the towers at high speed.

The towers had been hit from opposite directions, seventeen minutes apart, by planes moving at four hundred forty and five hundred ninety miles per hour and weighing perhaps a hundred tonnes each. The effect was catastrophic. Because the towers were built on the framed tube or "tube within a tube" design, the planes seriously damaged load-bearing columns at the perimeters, where they struck, and plowed through to the centers, also damaging the structural core. As if that wasn't enough, the tube-design acted like a pipe for the ten thousand gallons of jet fuel that spilled from each plane, flowing through and down the towers as it ignited and exploded. In the North Tower, the fuel also flooded into an elevator shaft, causing an explosion on the 22nd floor, far below the crash site.

The towers had been struck in different areas and and different speeds, leading to different effects in each case. Although the North Tower was the first to be hit, the South tower collapsed first. Kinetic energy – the energy of a moving object – is proportional to the square of the velocity, meaning that the second plane struck with a force roughly half as much again as the first. This led to significantly greater physical damage, before the effects of burning jet fuel were taken into account.

The hollow design of the building allowed the jet fuel to permeate deep into it, as well as down into the lower floors. It is possible that a more traditional type of skyscraper design might have prevented fuel and aircraft from penetrating as far as they did. Experts differ on the reasons the towers collapsed, but one thing they do agree on is the role of the fire. Thousands of gallons of jet fuel flooded into the tower at the collision points, traveling across the building and down the hollow centers and lift shafts. It burned briefly but fiercely, weakening the supportive core of the towers and damaging the flooring. After the fuel had burned out

– something that probably took no more than a few minutes – the contents of the towers continued to burn until their collapse.

The floors began to fall in before the superstructure gave out. In the South Tower, emergency services received a call from a man on the 105th floor, who told them that the lower floors were falling away – weakened by the crash and the fires, they dropped downwards, taking the floors below them with them on the way. It seems most likely that the sagging floors pulled the weakened support columns inwards until the structure finally succumbed to gravity and collapsed.

The event itself was a textbook example of progressive collapse. When the structural supports in the crash zone – already damaged by the impact – were catastrophically weakened by the fires, the intact section above them fell. The towers were designed to take enormous static loads, but a moving weight falling even a short distance would be disastrous due to the vastly multiplied forces involved. The top section remained intact until it hit the ground itself, but once the vertical collapse began, it was unstoppable.

Twenty-nine minutes later the North Tower collapsed. Radio failures meant that firefighters inside it had not realized that the South Tower had already fallen. Unlike in the South Tower, there was no escape for anyone above the collision line, since all the staircases had been severed. A total of three hundred forty-three firefighters died in the towers.

Some hours later, the World Trade Center – a forty-seven-story building in the complex – also collapsed. This time, the fall was a result of damage sustained from debris that hit it when the North Tower fell and the fires that were burning around the building. However, unlike the two major towers, evacuation was complete and there were miraculously no fatalities.

FIGHTING BACK

MEANWHILE, ON FLIGHT 93, the hijackers had begun their attack around forty-five minutes after take-off, taking the cockpit and redirecting the plane towards Washington DC. Their target was almost certainly the Capitol building. They captured the plane with relative ease, as the other terrorists had done in the other three planes, despite the fact they were a man down. Unlike the first three planes, on Flight 93 there were only four hijackers: the pilot, Al Qaeda member Ziad Jarrah, and three other 'muscle' hijackers, whose job it was to storm and secure the cockpit but who had not received the flight training necessary to redirect the plane to its target. It was also fortunate that the plane – a 757 – had a capacity of one hundred eighty-two passengers, but on this day was carrying only thirty-seven, plus seven crew members: the captain and first officer, and five flight attendants.

This time, the situation inside the plane was different. The forty-minute delay before the flight had left the asphalt had bought the passengers a little time. Not time to save themselves, but time to collect information on what was happening with the other three planes and to realize that they were part of the same plot. Instead of sit back and wait for the crash, which would kill themselves and perhaps hundreds or even thousands of other people on the ground, they decided to mount a counter-attack.

As soon as the seat belt sign had been turned off, the terrorists in first class made their move. Details are sketchy, but a certain amount has been pieced together from various sources, including cellphone calls and the cockpit flight recorder. In all, almost forty calls were made from passengers and staff on Flight 93. At least one passenger managed to stay connected to listeners on the ground the whole time until the plane crashed.

It appears that the hijackers' pilot, Jarrah, had remained in his seat whilst the other three set about securing the plane. Armed with knives (possibly no more than box cutters), they easily gained access to the cockpit. Investigators would later find a knife disguised as a cigarette lighter in the wreckage of the plane, indicating how small the blades were. The 9/11 Commission established that some of the hijackers had purchased Leatherman knives in the days beforehand. They were also armed with cans of mace or pepper spray. These, and some basic flight training, were the only tools that Al Qaeda used to wreak such untold devastation.

Sparsely armed though they were, it was all they needed. A Mayday transmission was received on the ground from the cockpit crew, followed by the words "Get out of here!" The passengers were moved to the back of the plane, and only when they were out of the way did Jarrah get up and take his seat at the controls. His first action was to speak to the passengers in passable but imperfect English, giving them the same line the other hijackers had done in order to frighten them into submission. "Ladies and gentlemen: here the captain, please sit down and keep remaining seating. We have a bomb on board. So sit." After changing course, he would tell them that they were on their way back to the airport in order to have their demands met.

At the back of the plane, hasty and hushed discussions were held. They had spoken to enough people on the ground and gleaned enough information about their hijackers to know that it was, in the words of one of them to his wife, a "suicide mission." There weren't any other options for them. It was a case of fighting back, no matter how small their chances of success, in the hope of regaining control of the plane and saving their own lives – or at the very least the lives of the people in their target – or waiting for the inevitable. Thirty minutes after the hijack had begun, the passengers began their counter-attack.

The small band of resistance was led by a man called Todd Beamer, a thirty-two-year-old account manager for Oracle who rose to the challenge and died a hero, spending the last few minutes of his life in a single-minded attempt to turn the tables against their captors. Beamer had a wife and two sons back in New Jersey, with a daughter on the way.

He tried to use his credit card to place a call from a phone at the back of the plane, but ended up being put through to a customer-service representative for the phone company, who connected him to a supervisor called Lisa Jefferson. Beamer told Jefferson what was going on, and that there had been at least one casualty – the hijackers had killed one of the passengers, and may have injured the pilot and co-pilot when they attacked them and threw them from the cockpit. While he was speaking, the plane banked sharply to the south-east as it re-routed towards its target. He left the call connected while the small group of passengers swiftly formulated their plan to re-take the plane. Before they began, he would tell Jefferson that they planned to jump on the hijackers and fly the plane into the ground before the terrorists could complete their attack.

Twenty-seven of the passengers had been told to sit in first class, whereas Beamer, nine other passengers and five flight attendants had been pushed into the back of the plane. Two of the hijackers remained in the cockpit with the pilot, whereas Beamer's group was guarded by the fourth: a man wearing a red belt that secured what appeared to be a bomb to his waist. In reality, this was certainly a decoy, intended only to scare the passengers into staying quiet. In any case, it didn't matter. Beamer and the others knew what the hijackers were planning. They could die in the air or die on the ground.

Finally, Beamer said the Lord's prayer with Jefferson, before putting the phone to one side. Jefferson would later say that the last words she heard Beamer say on the open line were, "Are you guys ready? Let's roll!"

It was three days later, on Friday September 14, that Lisa Jefferson kept her promise to call Todd Beamer's wife and tell her about what he had done. "It was the best thing that I could've gotten. It totally changed the mood around here," said Lisa Beamer. "We all knew what kind of person Todd was. We know he's in heaven. He was saved. Just knowing that when the crisis came up he maintained the same character we all knew, it's a testament to what real faith means. It's been a real uplift. It's put a spring in my step that I didn't have since Monday."

"That's Todd," his wife said, when she heard the call and his battle cry, "Let's roll!" played back. "My boys even say that. When we're getting ready to go somewhere, we say, 'C'mon guys, let's roll.' My little one says, 'C'mon, Mom, let's roll.' That's something they picked up from Todd." The words have become a national catchphrase, even becoming the title of a song about Beamer and Flight 93 by Neil Young.

What happened next on the plane isn't clear, but it seems that Beamer and the others managed to overpower their guard and rush to the front of the aircraft. As the band of passengers tried to storm the cockpit, Jarrah rolled the plane from side to side to try to knock them off balance, then rapidly moving the nose up and down. "They want to get in here. Hold, hold from the inside. Hold from the inside. Hold," he was heard to say to the other hijacker in the cockpit.

Realizing that their time was limited and that they would not reach their destination, the hijackers made the decision to down the plane, killing everyone on board. This seems to have been the passengers' intention, too. In a brief discussion they agreed to wait until the last possible moment, when the passengers were about to retake control. Jarrah was heard to say "Allāhu Akbar"

– "God is Great" several times – before pointing the nose of the plane downwards. Still the passengers continued their assault on the cockpit. It remains unclear whether Todd Beamer and his co-fighters had got back into the cockpit or were seconds away from doing so when the plane hit the ground, in a field in Stonycreek, Pennsylvania, around twenty minutes flight from their target. Jarrah appears to have flipped the plane onto its side or roof during the descent in order to ensure maximum devastation.

The plane plowed into the ground at five hundred sixty-three miles per hour at 10:03 a.m., upside-down and at almost a forty-five-degree angle. It gouged a scar ten feet deep and fifty feet long into a reclaimed coal strip mine in Stonycreek Township, a settlement of around two thousand people in Pennsylvania. Thanks to the location of the crash, no one on the ground was harmed.

A number of eyewitnesses saw the plane come down. One of them, Kelly Leverknight, had been following news reports of the other crashes when she heard the plane overhead. "I went out the front door and I saw the plane going down. It was headed toward the school, which panicked me, because all three of my kids were there. Then you heard the explosion and felt the blast and saw the fire and smoke."

Tim Thornsberg was working at a strip mine near the crash site. "It came in low over the trees and started wobbling. Then it just rolled over and was flying upside down for a few seconds… and then it kind of stalled and did a nose dive over the trees." Several other witnesses report seeing the plane flying fast and low, wobbling erratically before turning suddenly and sharply to the right and crashing. This must have been the moment at which Jarrah had realized they could no longer keep Beamer and the other passengers away from the controls, and had deliberately brought them down.

Eric Peterson saw the devastation of the crash. "It was low enough, I thought you could probably count the rivets. You could see more of the roof of the plane than you could the belly. It was on its side. There was a great explosion and you could see the flames. It was a massive, massive explosion. Flames and then smoke and then a massive, massive mushroom cloud."

The impact took down local electricity and phone connections and the force of the smash carried debris up to eight miles from the crash site. This, amongst other details, would later be used by conspiracy theorists to support the idea that the plane had been shot down. The suggestion was that decompression caused the contents of the airplane to be sucked from the hole, scattering them over a wide area. At least one of the witnesses to the crash claims that she was told – privately – by law enforcement officials that this is what happened.

Such an idea was not outside the bounds of possibility. One of the hardest decisions President Bush had to make, after being hurried from the school into Air Force One by Secret Service, was to decide what the response should be if the fighter patrols that had just been scrambled encountered unresponsive passenger jets. In a hasty phone conversation with the Vice President, Bush realized that – politically difficult though it was – the alternative was far worse. If an aircraft was believed to be under the control of hijackers and was heading for a clear target, they had no option but to shoot it down. Another call to Donald Rumsfeld clarified what the rules of engagement should be.

"First, pilots would seek to make radio contact with the other plane and tell the pilot to land at a specific location," summarized the *Washington Post*. "If that failed, the pilots were to use visual signals. These included having the fighters fly in front of the other plane. If the plane continued heading toward what was seen as a significant target with apparently hostile intent, the U.S. pilot would have the authority to shoot it down."

Unbeknown to Todd Beamer and the others on the plane, as Flight 93 neared its target that is exactly what was happening. Cheney repeatedly authorized pilots to engage the aircraft. "It was obviously, a very significant action," Cheney later said. "You're asking American pilots to fire on a commercial airliner full of civilians. On the other hand, you had directly in front of me what had happened to the World Trade Center, and a clear understanding that once the plane was hijacked, it was a weapon." Just a few minutes later, reports came in that the plane had gone down, leading Bush to ask on Air Force One, "Did we shoot it down or did it crash?" It took two hours to establish that no contact had occurred between the fighter patrols and Flight 93.

Those two hours of doubt, and the tough but only reasonable decision reached by the White House, spawned the conspiracy theory that the plane had indeed been shot down by the U.S. But the details gleaned from the flight recorder and the various phone calls made from the plane by Beamer and his fellow passengers before the crash obviate the need for any such explanation. Knowing they were about to be robbed of their mission objective, Jarrah and the other hijackers settled for the next best thing: destroying the plane and all of its passengers rather than giving them the chance of capturing them alive and landing it safely. "I think an act of heroism occurred on board that plane," Cheney concluded, as they tried to make sense of what had happened.

The aircraft hit the ground with such force that it was pulverized, smashing into fragments that shattered everything around them. So great was the impact and the subsequent explosion that hardly any human remains could be discerned, let alone identified by sight. There was no way of knowing who had been alive and who had already been dead when the crash happened. Piecing together the final moments before the crash would require painstaking work on the part of the emergency services, and would require a sustained period of time.

The last plane was down, less than two hours after the hijacks had begun. The immediate damage was done, with almost 3,000 dead. The rescue work would continue throughout the day and for several more to come. Ground Zero, as it became known, was not fully cleared until May 2002.

CONCLUSION: AFTERMATH

"The Pearl Harbor of
the 21st Century"

9/11 REVERBERATED AROUND the world and will continue to do so for decades to come. The hours and days after the four planes crashed were a whirl of panic-stricken activity, as U.S. officials worked to establish who was responsible for the atrocities, and what their response should be.

At 11:30 in the evening of the attacks, President Bush wrote in his diary: "The Pearl Harbor of the 21st century took place today. We think it's Osama bin Laden. We think there are other targets in the United States, but I have urged the country to go back to normal. We cannot allow a terrorist thug to hold us hostage. My hope is that this will provide an opportunity for us to rally the world against terrorism."

There had been chatter in the intelligence network for months that bin Laden was planning an attack on the United States. One of the events that would later take its place as one of the larger pieces in the jigsaw of evidence was the arrest of Zacarias Moussaoui, who had taken flight training in the same school as two of the 9/11 pilots, Mohammed Atta and Marwan al-Shehhi. Atta and al-Shehhi would finally fly the two Boeings into the North and South Towers of the World Trade Center; Moussaoui failed his training and was never allowed to fly a plane solo. He was arrested in August 2001 for an immigration violation. CIA director George J. Tenet was heard to muse, in the first minutes after the attacks: "I wonder if it has anything to do with this guy taking pilot training." Moussaoui's connection to 9/11 is open to question; it is quite possible that he was involved in a separate plot, possibly one of his own devising. Nevertheless, this was one of many strands of evidence that could have led back to bin Laden and his intentions to carry out a major plot against the U.S. Tenet knew something was about to happen; he just didn't know what or where. As soon as the attacks occurred, he told one of his close friend, former Senator David Boren, "This has bin Laden all over it."

For what it was worth, bin Laden initially denied his part in bankrolling and planning the atrocities, using his statement to turn the knife against the U.S. for its own perceived injustices in the Middle East. "I have already said that I am not involved in the September 11, attacks in the United States. As a Muslim, I try my best to avoid telling a lie. I had no knowledge of these attacks, nor do I consider the killing of innocent women, children and other humans as an appreciable act. Islam strictly forbids causing harm to innocent women, children and other people. Such a practice is forbidden even in the course of a battle. It is the United States, which is perpetrating every maltreatment on women, children and common people of other faiths, particularly the followers of Islam. All that is going on in Palestine for the last 11 months is sufficient to call the wrath of God upon the United States and Israel. There is also a warning for those Muslim countries, which witnessed all these as a silent spectator. What had earlier been done to the innocent people of Iraq, Chechnya and Bosnia? Only one conclusion could be derived from the indifference of the United States and the West to these acts of terror and the patronage of the tyrants by these powers that America is an anti-Islamic power and it is patronizing the anti-Islamic forces. Its friendship with the Muslim countries is just a show, rather deceit. By enticing or intimidating these countries, the United States is forcing them to play a role of its choice. Put a glance all around and you will see that the slaves of the United States are either rulers or enemies of Muslims."

This was the statement apparently made by Osama bin Laden to *Ummat*, an Islamist Pakistani newspaper and published on 28 September 28, 2001, two-and-a-half weeks after the attacks. The defense continued: "According to my information, the death toll is much higher than what the U.S. Government has stated. But the Bush Administration does not want the panic to spread. The United States should try to trace the perpetrators of these attacks within itself; the people who are a part of the U.S. system, but are dissenting against it. Or those who are working for some other system; persons who want to make the present century as a century of conflict between Islam and Christianity so that their own civilization, nation, country, or ideology could survive. They can be anyone, from Russia to Israel and from India to Serbia. In the U.S. itself, there are dozens of well-organized and well-equipped groups, which are capable of causing a large-scale destruction. Then you cannot forget the American-Jews, who are annoyed with President Bush ever since the elections in Florida and want to avenge him. Then there are intelligence agencies in the U.S., which require billions of dollars worth of funds from the Congress and the government every year. This [funding issue] was not a big problem till the existence of the former Soviet Union but after that the budget of these agencies has been in danger. They needed an enemy. So, they first started propaganda against Osama and Taleban and then this incident happened."

The statement was reminiscent of the conspiracy theories that would sprout on American soil: that the 9/11 attacks were either part of an anti-government plot within the U.S., or even part of the administration itself, designed to justify their budgets, powers and intentions. However, the *Ummat* report was later discredited on the grounds that the interviewer had not spoken in person to bin Laden: he had simply sent a written list of questions to Taliban leaders in Afghanistan, who had sent back their answers. At the time, Afghanistan was facing invasion from the U.S. and such denial was only to be expected as a delay or propaganda tactic.

Although there was little doubt in the minds of the U.S. authorities, bin Laden did not categorically admit his responsibility for another three years. He had come close in one message, released the day before the second anniversary of the attacks, on September 10, 2003. In an accompanying video, he walks with Ayman al-Zawahiri – now the new head of Al Qaeda – through the mountains, both carrying assault rifles. In the taped message he praised the damage done to "the enemy," mentioning five of the hijackers by name. But this endorsement fell short of his admission of direct guilt.

It was more than a year later, in October 2004, that he finally spoke of his participation. It was apparently an opportunistic statement, made just days before the presidential election and assuring Americans that their safety could only be secured if they stopped persecuting Muslims. He criticized the outgoing president, George W. Bush, for misleading the U.S. and said that the same conditions that prompted 9/11 still existed, meaning that "there are still reasons to repeat what happened."

"Your security is not in the hands of Kerry, Bush or Al Qaeda. Your security is in your own hands," *Fox News* quoted him. "Any state that does not mess with our security, has naturally guaranteed its own security." He said that the 9/11 attacks had been his reparation for injustices by Americans and Israel against the Lebanese and Palestinians.

"In what appeared to be conciliatory language, bin Laden said he wanted to explain why he ordered the airline hijackings that hit the World Trade Center and the Pentagon so Americans would know how to act to prevent another attack. "To the American people, my talk is to you about the best way to avoid another Manhattan," he said. "I tell you: security is an important element of human life and free people do not give up their security." The video also served as confirmation that bin Laden was alive and well, and still a serious threat to the U.S.

The War on Terror

By 2004, HIS CATEGORICAL involvement was old news to the U.S. Key officials suspected within minutes of the terrorist attacks that bin Laden was the ringleader, and reacted accordingly.

When he learned that the first plane had crashed into the North Tower, Bush had assumed that it was a tragic accident. "This is pilot error," he remembers saying to his Chief of Staff, at a snatched moment out of earshot of the pupils at the elementary school he was visiting. "It's unbelievable that somebody would do this. The guy must have had a heart attack." With news of the second impact, he instantly changed his mind. "They had declared war on us, and I made up my mind at that moment that we were going to war," he recalls thinking.

A fast response was essential, but it couldn't be organized overnight. Rumsfeld warned that military action would take two months to arrange. Sitting in the PEOC – the Presidential Emergency Operations Center, the bunker beneath the White House – Bush considered the options with his advisors. "This is the time for self-defense," he said. "We have made the decision to punish whoever harbors terrorists, not just the perpetrators."

That meant military strikes against countries who sheltered Al Qaeda. Perhaps the biggest question was where to start. They needed firm evidence to determine the country most closely associated with the terrorists. Afghanistan was the most obvious place, but there were no fewer than sixty countries with connections to bin Laden. ("Let's pick them off one at a time," Bush had suggested.)

It was five days later that Bush first used the phrase that would encapsulate America's response to 9/11. Addressing the cameras at Camp David, he warned, "This crusade – this war on terrorism – is going to take a while. And the American people must be patient. I'm going to be patient. But I can assure the American people I am determined."

Nine days after the attacks, the considerable questions around America's response to the attacks had largely been settled. The war was announced on September 20, in a televised address to a joint session of congress. "Our war on terror begins with Al Qaeda, but it does not end there. It will not end until every terrorist group of global reach has been found, stopped and defeated."

The War on Terror in earnest began less than four weeks after 9/11 with the launch of Operation Enduring Freedom. Its aim: to destroy Al Qaeda in Afghanistan, removing the Taliban regime that sheltered and endorsed it and bringing democracy to the country. The U.S. were assisted by British Special Forces and the Afghan Northern Alliance – a collection of Afghan groups fighting against the Taliban and Al Qaeda. Beginning with massive air strikes, the operation succeeded in dismantling the Taliban within weeks, scattering them and forcing many to flee into Pakistan and the mountainous region between the two countries.

Bin Laden himself fled to this inhospitable area, where he narrowly escaped death at the hands of the U.S. forces in December 2001. His youngest wife, Amal, spoke to a Saudi magazine, *Al Majalla*, about those early days after 9/11. "When the U.S. bombing of Afghanistan started, we moved to a mountainous area with some children and lived in one of the caves for two months until one of his sons came with a group of tribesmen and took us with them," *Time* quoted her. She says she was later moved back to Yemen with the help of Pakistani officials. She would ultimately end up back in Pakistan, in the Abbottabad compound where bin Laden was killed. She told the magazine that she was not a part of any of these decisions – she was simply taken one day. "I did not know that we were going to Pakistan until they handed us over to the Pakistani government."

Initial estimates of the death toll from 9/11 were around six thousand, until the figure was eventually revised downwards to just under three thousand. Even then, there was a terrible sense of outraged disbelief, that such an act could have been perpetrated against civilians by terrorists on American soil. Something had to be done, and it had to be done quickly. Bush's approval ratings spiked to ninety percent with his uncompromising response to 9/11 – though, by the end of his second term, it had dropped to just twenty-five percent, the lowest of any recent president except Richard Nixon.

One of the factors that led to that drop in approval, at least in the short term (the response to Hurricane Katrina, the prolonged Iraq War, and economic meltdown were more recent problems) was the discovery, some months after 9/11, that the CIA had told Bush of an impending threat several weeks before it actually happened.

There had been questions about the responses of government agencies to intelligence gathered about the possible threat. At the beginning of May 2002, it was reported than an FBI agent had realized that one flight school was receiving an unusually high number of Arab men applying for pilot training. He had submitted a memo to the Bureau, mentioning bin Laden by name and recommending that the FBI check all flight schools in the U.S. with the intention of identifying potential terrorists. The FBI did not consider the memo worth acting upon. They also came in for heavy criticism for the way they had treated Zacarias Moussaoui, who had failed flight training and been arrested for immigration offenses prior to 9/11. Later questioning of this possible candidate for the identity of "20th hijacker" turned up many useful leads and links to Al Qaeda; a more prompt and thorough investigation might have led to information that could have been used to prevent the attacks. It was no certainty, by any stretch, but it was a line of inquiry that could have been fruitful. "It represents a failure to connect the dots," said a spokesman for the Senate Select Committee on Intelligence. "This was dismissed rather lightly at FBI headquarters."

However, in mid-May 2002 it came out that the CIA had actually warned President Bush in person that something like this could happen – reigniting the debate that the attacks could have been prevented if action had been taken. On holiday at his ranch in Texas, Bush was told in an intelligence briefing that it was possible that Al Qaeda were planning to hijack American planes – although there was no suggestion that they might be crashed into buildings. "There has been longstanding speculation, shared with the president, about the potential of hijackings in the traditional sense," admitted White House press secretary, Ari Fleischer. "We had general threats involving Osama bin Laden around the world and including in the United States."

The public was never told about this possibility, and Fleischer stated that the government had notified all the appropriate agencies – though he could not say which agencies had been warned, or what they had been told. Nevertheless, he claims, this action was the reason that the hijackers had to use such unsophisticated means to take control of the planes. "I think that's one of the reasons that we saw the people who committed the September 11 attacks used box cutters and plastic knives to get around America's system of protecting against hijackers." This was a hollow defense; whatever measure were taken, box cutters were enough.

Against the backdrop of Congress's investigation into whether 9/11 could have been prevented, this did not look good. After the ratings bump of retaliatory action in Afghanistan, Bush experienced a gradual but sustained decline in popularity – boosted briefly by military action against Iraq and the capture of Saddam Hussein – as the War on Terror took its toll against America in thousands of casualties. Bin Laden's plot had achieved more for Al Qaeda than the deaths on American soil; it had led to many further deaths and injuries, and badly undermined the Bush administration in the long term.

In some quarters, these concerns about the competence of the government gave way to full-blown conspiracy theory, with proponents alleging everything in the spectrum between the idea that Bush had covered up the incompetence that allowed the attacks to happen, through knowing about the plot in advance and letting it proceed anyway, to the extreme fringe that elements of the U.S. government were actually directly responsible for 9/11. In the latter case, it is posited that they either collaborated with Al Qaeda or simply framed them as a convenient scapegoat afterwards.

There are many variants, with numerous justifications – frequently the creation of a pretext to invade the Middle East in order to control oil interests. One of the most popular is that the twin towers of the World Trade Center did not collapse due to the impact of the aircraft, but in a controlled demolition. These theories typically arose some time after the events, as apparent discrepancies and inconsistencies in the accounts emerged, along with details of the miscommunication and unexpected inaction from and between government agencies such as the CIA and FBI.

The problem is that there is strong evidence for some kind of bad judgment or poor communication between agencies that did raise the probability of the 9/11 attacks proceeding unchecked. Coleen Rowley is a former FBI agent who turned whistleblower after the event to uncover some of the loose ends that had been ignored. Writing in the *LA Times*, she raised the specter of Moussaoui – a recurring theme in the investigation that eventually occurred. "Following up on a tip from flight school instructors who had become suspicious of the French Moroccan who claimed to want to fly a jet as an ego boost, Special Agent Harry

Samit and an INS colleague had detained Moussaoui. A foreign intelligence service promptly reported that he had connections with a foreign terrorist group, but FBI officials in Washington inexplicably turned down Samit's request for authority to search Moussaoui's laptop computer and personal effects.

"Those same officials stonewalled Samit's supervisor, who pleaded with them in late August 2001 that he was 'trying to keep someone from taking a plane and crashing into the World Trade Center.' (Yes, he was that explicit.) Later, testifying at Moussaoui's trial, Samit testified that he believed the behavior of his FBI superiors in Washington constituted "criminal negligence." The 9/11 Commission ultimately concluded that Moussaoui was most likely being primed as a Sept.11 replacement pilot and that the hijackers probably would have postponed their strike if information about his arrest had been announced."

Rowley's co-author in the *LA Times* was Federal Air Marshal Bogdan Dzakovic, who before 9/11 led the FAA's 'Red Team' – a group that conducted vulnerability testing in airport security. "He also has a story of how warnings were ignored in the run-up to Sept. 11. In repeated tests of security, his team found weaknesses nine out of 10 times that would make it possible for hijackers to smuggle weapons aboard and seize control of airplanes. But the team's reports were ignored and suppressed, and the team was shut down entirely after 9/11.

"In testimony to the 9/11 Commission, Dzakovic summed up his experience this way: 'The Red Team was extraordinarily successful in killing large numbers of innocent people in the simulated attacks...[and yet] we were ordered not to write up our reports and not to retest airports where we found particularly egregious vulnerabilities.... Finally, the FAA started providing advance notification of when we would be conducting our "undercover" tests and what we would be checking.'"

These types of criticisms, along with more direct accusations of conspiracy theory, form the basis of the so-called '9/11 Truth' movement. Its flagship website, *911truth.org*, states that its purpose is "To expose the official lies and cover-up surrounding the events of September 11, 2001 in a way that inspires the people to overcome denial and understand the truth; namely, that elements within the U.S. government and covert policy apparatus must have orchestrated or participated in the execution of the attacks for these to have happened in the way that they did."

The movement has drawn support from a number of high-profile figures. One of the most famous – or infamous – of these is Michael Moore, whose documentary movie *Fahrenheit 9/11* was hugely influential. In it, Moore details – amongst other things – the long-standing links between the Bush and bin Laden family, the U.S. government, the Saudi government and the Taliban. Based on the findings of the 9/11 Commission, he stated that "After the airspace reopened, six chartered flights with 142 people, mostly Saudi Arabian nationals, departed from the United States between September 14 and 24. One flight, the so-called bin Laden flight, departed the United States on September 20 with 26 passengers, most of them relatives of Osama bin Laden." They received no more than a brief interview from U.S. officials before leaving.

Two other major strands to the conspiracy theorists' cases are the ideas that speculators benefited enormously from short-selling shares in stocks that were about to plunge, suggesting foreknowledge, and that the World Trade Center could not have collapsed due to the impact of the planes and jet fuel fires, but must have been rigged with explosives beforehand.

All of these theories have rational explanations and have been argued by academics and journalists on the opposite side *ad infinitum*. All the same, conspiracy theories are enduring and dearly loved by a surprisingly large minority of the U.S. population, as well as many abroad.

The following war liberated Afghanistan from the Taliban relatively quickly, and bin Laden was forced into hiding by the relentless efforts of U.S. and coalition military – narrowly escaping death in the mountains of Tora Bora on at least one occasion. That was the last time he was seen for more than nine years. He continued to release video messages at sporadic intervals, but his location was never clear – until August 2010, when the CIA finally tracked his courier to Abbottabad. Still, the war in Afghanistan rumbled on for more than a decade after the initial invasion, the transition to democracy occurring fitfully.

Bin Laden had handed President Bush a poisoned chalice with the 9/11 attacks, and nothing is more symptomatic of this than the Iraq War. Seen as "the central front in the War on Terror," the Bush administration argued that Iraq had to be invaded as a state sponsor of Al Qaeda. The claim that Iraq had weapons of mass destruction at its disposal became the lynch-pin of the argument. Initially praised for his decision to take down Saddam Hussein, Bush soon found himself mired isycontroversy, as the U.S. found itself unable to leave the country without causing a dangerous vacuum that would likely be filled by extremists.

Two of the most significant claims were made by Vice President Cheney in the early days after 9/11. One was that Iraq was sheltering one of the suspects from the 1993 World Trade Center bombing. "We learned more and more that there was a relationship between Iraq and Al Qaida that stretched back through most of the decade of the '90s, that it involved training, for example... that Al Qaida sent personnel to Baghdad to get trained on the systems that are involved. The Iraqis providng bomb-making expertise and advice to the Al Qaida organization. We know, for example, in connection with the original World Trade Center bombing in '93 that one of the bombers was Iraqi, returned to Iraq after the attack of '93. And we've learned subsequent to that, since we went into Baghdad and got into the intelligence files, that this individual probably also received financing from the Iraqi government as well as safe haven."

More significantly, Cheney stated that there was probably a direct link between Saddam and Mohammed Atta, the ringleader of the 9/11 hijackers. "With respect to 9/11, of course, we've had the story that's been public out there. The Czechs alleged that Mohamed Atta, the lead attacker, met in Prague with a senior Iraqi intelligence official five months before the attack, but we've never been able to develop any more of that yet either in terms of confirming it or discrediting it. We just don't know."

A year after the attacks, Donald Rumsfeld stated that there was 'bulletproof' evidence that Al Qaeda was linked to Saddam Hussein. He could not offer details without endangering his sources, he said, acknowledging that the evidence would not stand up in court. "If our quest is for proof positive, we probably will be left somewhat unfulfilled... We're not going to have everything beyond a reasonable doubt." But the case was building. A week earlier Bush had warned of the possibility "that Al Qaeda becomes an extension of Saddam's madness." By February 2003, just before the War in Iraq, two-thirds of Americans believed there was a link between bin Laden and Saddam Hussein.

It would later emerge that there was no credible evidence directly linking Saddam to Al Qaeda or the terrorist attacks on September 11 – something Bush admitted in 2006. In fact, there is also strong evidence that bin Laden heavily mistrusted Saddam and hated him as a secularist whose regime was anathema with his own brand of political Islam. When Iraq invaded Kuwait in 1990, bin Laden offered to help in the fight against Saddam by sending his own mujahideen (an offer that was refused).

In 1999, bin Laden had reiterated his warnings about Saddam. "A year before Hussein entered Kuwait, I said many times in my speeches at the mosques, warning that Saddam will enter the Gulf. No one believed me. I distributed many tapes in Saudi Arabia. It was after it happened that they started believing me and believed my analysis of the situation." Peter Bergen, author of *The Osama bin Laden I Know*, quoted another source close to him, Khaled Batarfi. "Last time I saw Osama was 1990, six months before the Iraqi invasion of Kuwait. It was in Mecca, in a friend's house, where a group of intellectuals meet every Friday. And he came and talked about jihad in Afghanistan and told us then that he'd speak to us about Saddam. He said, 'We should train our people, our young, and increase our army and prepare for the day when eventually we are attacked. This guy [Saddam] can never be trusted.' He doesn't believe Saddam is a Muslim. So he never liked him or trusted him." A stronger statement about bin Laden's views on Saddam was given by his Pakistani biographer, Hamid Mir, who spoke to bin Laden about Saddam in 1997. "He condemned Saddam Hussein in my interview. He gave such kind of abuses that it was very difficult for me to write, [calling Hussein a] socialist motherf***er. 'The land of the Arab world, the land is like a mother, and Saddam Hussein is f***ing his mother.' He also explained that Saddam Hussein is against us, and he discourages Iraqi boys to come to Afghanistan."

No Going Back

PART OF BIN LADEN'S legacy has been to blur the lines between truth and lies, casting doubt on the perceived integrity of those who responded to his terrorist atrocities by implicitly questioning the grounds on which they acted. Time and again, critics have warned that the abuses that have resulted from the West's reaction to bin Laden were worse than the original crimes. In extreme cases, they claim that those reactions have actually increased terrorism, since they serve as a powerful recruiting tool to Al Qaeda.

Beyond the thousands of casualties, direct and indirect, that resulted from bin Laden's reign of terror, this is his legacy: the forcing of a moral compromise that has made the world a worse place through the very means by which we tried to make it better. No one disagrees that the attacks of September 11 – or any of bin Laden's other terrorist attacks – were evil. No one disagrees that swift and decisive action was imperative to stop further atrocities. But somehow, that imperative has forced a Catch-22 situation where – whatever the response – freedoms are lost.

Only a month after 9/11, Amnesty International warned of some of the unintended consequences in other countries. "In the name of fighting "international terrorism," governments have rushed to introduce draconian new measures that threaten the human rights of their own citizens, immigrants and refugees… Governments have a responsibility to ensure the safety of their citizens, but measures taken must not undermine fundamental human rights standards. It appears that some of the initiatives currently being discussed or implemented may be used to curb basic human rights and to suppress internal opposition. Some of the definitions of terrorism under discussion are so broad that they could be used to criminalize anyone out of favor with those in power and criminalize legitimate peaceful exercise of the right to freedom of expression and association. They could also put at risk the right to privacy and threaten the rights of minorities and asylum-seekers."

This warning was reiterated in 2003, when two new wars had taken their toll. "The war on terror, far from making the world a safer place, has made it more dangerous by curtailing human rights, undermining the rule of international law and shielding governments from scrutiny. It has deepened divisions among people of different faiths and origins, sowing the seeds for more conflict. The overwhelming impact of all this is genuine fear – among the affluent as well as the poor."

9/11 – and the response to it – galvanized Islamic terrorists, and in the last decade there have been around two dozen major attacks or attempts, including the July 7, 2005 bombings in London and the 2002 nightclub bombings in Bali. Al Qaeda was never a centralized organization, and some of the attacks of the last ten years occurred without top-down consent or planning; indeed, there have been a number of attacks (usually unsuccessful) that were the work of loners, or small groups of radicalized Muslims working independently, without connection to wider networks and resources. In the internet age, anyone can gain the information they need to become a terrorist.

So far, in a state of heightened alert and with all the resources of the most powerful country in the world, the U.S. has generally stayed ahead of the terrorists. For every successful attack there are three or four that are foiled. And yet, a question mark still hangs over Al Qaeda. Bin Laden is dead, but his legacy lives on.

Following the SEALs' raid on bin Laden's compound, Al Qaeda sources have vowed revenge. On May 13, less than two weeks after he was shot and killed, two Pakistani suicide bombers killed eighty people in Shabqadar, a market town in northwest Pakistan. It was a classic bin Laden operation, combining uncompromising devotion to the cause with ruthless strategy. Eight hundred soldiers had just graduated from the training academy in the town. As they left their base at 6 A.M., the first suicide bomber walked up to them and detonated his explosives. The second waited eight minutes, while hundreds more troops rushed to tend the wounded, until detonating his own. The bomb vests had been packed with ball bearings, scything out under the force of the explosives like a huge shotgun cartridge and devastating the crowd around them. eighty people died and a further one hundred twenty were wounded. This, said the Taliban, was just the first installment of the 'blood price' they had vowed would be paid in return for bin Laden's death.

Reuters quoted one Taliban Afghan shortly after the raid. "Now he is the number one martyr for Al Qaeda because he is stronger dead than alive. He always predicted that he would be killed by Americans. Now he will become a fire that Muslims will follow for generations." The danger is that this is exactly what will happen, since Al Qaeda did not rely on bin Laden's leadership and has plenty of other leaders just as dangerous – or even more so – than their late figurehead.

And yet this is by no means certain. In the days and weeks following bin Laden's death further Al Qaeda leaders and operatives have been targeted and killed – some as a direct result of the intelligence gathered from his compound, others simply coincidentally. Ilyas Kashmiri was a senior figure in Al Qaeda, tipped as one possible replacement for bin Laden. He had trained the mujahideen in Afghanistan in the 1980s, losing an eye and a finger in the fighting. In later years, he was associated with a number of significant terrorist plots, whether executed or merely planned, including the Camp Chapman attack in December 2009 that killed seven CIA operatives and seriously injured six others. Kashmiri was killed in a strike by a U.S. drone on 3 June, 2011 in a Taliban-controlled area of South Waziristan, along with eight other militants. There has been widespread speculation that the strike was enabled by information gathered from bin Laden's compound. A week later, Fazul Abdullah Mohammed, the leader of Al Qaeda in East Africa, was killed when he failed to stop at a checkpoint near Mogadishu, Somalia. Secretary of State Hillary Clinton called the event "a significant blow to Al Qaeda, its extremist allies and its operations in East Africa."

The future may be uncertain, but there is the sense that the fight against Al Qaeda is accelerating and that, following bin Laden's death, more senior figures are being mopped up. Moreover, in the light of the Arab Spring, a question mark has appeared over the relevance of organizations like Al Qaeda that attempt to force change through violent jihad. This new movement, sweeping the Arab world, must have stunned bin Laden as it threatened the entire *raison d'être* of the group to which he had devoted his life.

And what of bin Laden himself? There are plenty of conspiracy theories out there about his 'disappearance' in the light of his swift burial and Obama's refusal to release any photos of his corpse. One is that he has been removed to a top-secret 'black site' and is being interrogated about the possibility that Al Qaeda has access to a nuclear weapon, as Khalid Sheikh Mohammed claimed. If this were true, any interrogation that took place would make KSM's own waterboarding marathon at the hands of the CIA look like a picnic.

But conspiracy theorists will always have their day and their ideas rarely bear up to close scrutiny. Whatever loose ends remain around the account of his death, and around the future of the organization he founded in Afghanistan in the late 1980s, bin Laden's own story was decisively ended by the two teams of Navy SEALs who raided his hiding place in Abbottabad,

Pakistan, almost a decade after the worst terrorist atrocities in American history.

Perhaps he really is enjoying Paradise and the rewards that martyrs are traditionally believed to receive in the afterlife. But the truth is likely more prosaic: an anonymous grave at the bottom of the North Arabian Sea and a fast-closing chapter in the history books of the late 20th and early 21st centuries. Whether justice comes in merely earthly terms or has eternal implications, it was served for Osama bin Laden on May 1, 2011.

POSTSCRIPT: THE ARAB SPRING AND THE FUTURE OF AL QAEDA

MOHAMED BOUAZIZI WAS an unremarkable twenty-six-year-old Tunisian man. His father had died when he was three and his mother's second husband, also his uncle, was unable to support the family due to poor health. His home town, Sidi Bouzid, had unemployment rates of around thirty percent – three times higher than America's at the height of the recession brought about by the global financial crisis. Bouazizi did what he could to support his family by selling fruit and vegetables on the street.

Sidi Bouzid was, like many other towns of Tunisia, known for its corrupt officials. Bouazizi is reported to have suffered for years at the hands of the police, who regularly confiscated his produce. This was once again the case on December 17, 2010, when officials took his scales and overturned his wheelbarrow on the grounds that he did not have a street vendor's permit. No such permit is required for those selling from such a cart, and his family have stated that the years of abuse were a result of his inability to afford to pay bribes to police to leave him alone. In this case, he had so little money that he had had to buy his produce on credit, and its confiscation left him with a two hundred dollar debt.

The official at the center of the incident was Faida Hamdi, a forty-five-year-old female municipal inspector and the daughter of a police officer. She is reported to have slapped Bouazizi and spat in his face, also insulting his dead father, while her companions beat him. In the conservative Tunisian society in which it occurred, his public humiliation was all the worse for him because it happened at the hands of a woman. Bouazizi went straight to the mayor's office to complain and retrieve his scales, but he was turned away.

He had exhausted what few small opportunities for justice existed for him. Desperate and with nowhere else to turn, he obtained a can of gasoline and stood in the middle of traffic outside the governor's office. Dousing himself with the gas, the anguished young man shouted "How do you expect me to make a living?" and set himself alight.

Self-immolation, as it is known, is a hideous, agonizing form of suicide. In has long been known in the region as a statement of political protest: a form of public and dramatic martyrdom carried out when, as it was for Bouazizi, all other chances of restitution have been denied. Unlike the suicide bombers used by bin Laden and other extremist groups, their purpose is to highlight intractable injustice by inflicting immense personal suffering without harming anyone else.

Bouazizi died from his injuries eighteen days later in the hospital, but his actions sparked a larger fire across Tunisia and the Middle East. His death became a touchstone for all those who had no voice against the many injustices they experienced on a daily basis: corruption, poverty, unemployment, political oppression and high food prices. The protests that his death catalyzed led to the end of the Tunisian regime, with President Zine El Abidine Ben Ali fleeing the country in January 2011. Enabled by mobile phones and social networking sites, popular protests began in Egypt, culminating eighteen days later with the end of Hosni Mubarak's long presidency. Libya and Syria soon experienced prolonged, widespread and violent anti-government protests, with other countries' citizens expressing various degrees of unrest and anger at their treatment: Yemen, Iraq, Algeria, Morocco and others across the Middle East and North Africa.

This spontaneous wave of grass-roots revolt is fundamentally opposed to bin Laden's guiding intention. Al Qaeda played no part in the reforms that have been demanded and – with varying degrees of success to date – achieved. The people of the Middle East do not want bin Laden's vision of a true Muslim Caliphate. They want open, fair democracy. As *Time* magazine observed, "During these past few months of momentous political upheaval in the Middle East, Al Qaeda's leaders were barely seen or heard. Their feeble attempts to claim a role in unshackling Arabs from their decades-old, repressive (and largely pro-American) regimes were ignored. In many ways, Osama bin Laden and his band of extremist brothers were already largely irrelevant in this region long before news of the terror mastermind's death in Pakistan. The movement was marginalized and 'little more than a symbol as a result of his past achievements,' as Peter Harling, a Middle East analyst with the International Crisis Group, told *TIME*." The ideal that bin Laden was trying to establish was, in fact, unpalatable and undesirable to a large proportion of Arabs.

Bin Laden's death was a significant, but not fatal blow to Al Qaeda. His replacement lacks bin Laden's ability to enthuse and recruit, whatever his operational experience as a jihadi. A more significant threat to the organization's future is its diminishing relevance. In the future world brought about by the Arab Spring, Al Qaeda's place is increasingly marginalized. The next generation of Arabs, tired of their parents' autocratic, oppressive rulers and the corrupt regimes over which they preside, have no interest in either dictatorship or extremism as organizing forces. Bin Laden must have recognized this as the protests spread across the region during the last few months of his life, realizing that his ideology had no place in the world to come. His death, a pounding disappointment to Al Qaeda's collective identity, can only have been a reflection of his own disillusionment that his life's mission had been in vain: young, educated Arabs had looked to his generation and firmly decided that their own children would not be subject to the same mistakes that they were. From that perspective, his death in Abbottabad five months into the Arab Spring was fitting, because it marks the end of an era. Olivier Roy, an expert on Islamic militancy, comments: "It's certainly coincidence that the two events are linked in time, but in fact it's logical because the death of bin Laden symbolized the marginalization of Al Qaeda in the Middle East."

Alongside his death, and that marginalization of the organization he founded and steered for more than two decades, comes the hope of lasting change – not as a result of jihad, but of democracy, one of the very things that bin Laden so hated about the West.

BIBLIOGRAPHY

Peter Bergen, 2006. *The Osama bin Laden I Know An Oral History of Al Qaeda's Leader* (Winnipeg: Free Press).

Steve Coll, 2008. *The bin Ladens: An Arabian Family in the American Century* (New York: Penguin Press HC).

Omar bin Laden, Najwa bin Laden and Jean Sasson, 2009. *Growing Up bin Laden* (New York: St. Martin's Press).

Richard Miniter, 2003. *Losing bin Laden: How Bill Clinton's Failures Unleashed Global Terror* (Washington DC: Regnery Publishing).

Lawrence Wright, 2006. *The Looming Tower: Al Qaeda and the Road to 9/11* (New York: Knopf).